Alcohol and Tobacco Tax and Trade Bureau

ANNUAL
REPORT

FISCAL YEAR 2013

Table of Contents

Introduction

Supporting the Nation's economic vitality is at the core of the work performed by the Alcohol and Tobacco Tax and Trade Bureau (TTB). The Bureau's role in permitting and regulating the alcohol and tobacco industries ensures a fair marketplace, enhanced trade opportunities, and a level playing field for those engaged in the manufacture and trade of these commodities. As the Nation's excise tax authority on alcohol and tobacco products, TTB also ensures fair and effective tax administration and enforcement in a globalized marketplace.

TTB is focused on supporting the business community it serves by reducing the burden of compliance and addressing the illicit trade that undermines their legitimate operations. In the 10 years since TTB's inception, the industries that the Bureau regulates have continued to expand, evidenced by the 60 percent growth in the permit applications and registrations that TTB receives. Annual tax revenue from the alcohol, tobacco, firearms, and ammunition industries totals approximately $23 billion annually, making TTB the third largest tax collection agency in the federal government. The revenue that TTB collects on these products funds national priorities.

Maintaining a responsive and effective organization requires Government agencies to look at their business processes and operations anew. TTB, like the businesses it regulates, must continuously look for ways to effect its mandates more efficiently and effectively, leveraging limited resources in smarter and more innovative ways to ensure that the investments made in its mission achieve a positive return. Within its FY 2013 Annual Report, TTB combines program performance with financial data to demonstrate how effectively the Bureau translates its program dollars into quality service, responsible management practices, consumer protection, and increased tax revenue.

Each year, as part of the performance and budget cycle, TTB issues this report to inform its stakeholders of the Bureau's accomplishments and explain any challenges. The report defines the Bureau's mission, strategic goals, and major programs, and summarizes its progress in meeting its objectives, as stated in the TTB strategic plan. TTB also presents financial information that depicts how TTB expended its budget according to its major programs, and accounted for tax collections from the alcohol, tobacco, firearms, and ammunition industries.

This report presents this information in four parts:

Part I – Management's Discussion and Analysis. This section provides an overview of the Bureau, including its mission and programs, highlights of program and financial operations, and a summary of TTB's program performance.

Part II – Program Performance Results. This section provides a discussion of results achieved for each performance measure related to the Collect the Revenue and Protect the Public strategic goals and an overview of the Bureau's accomplishments under its Management and Organizational Excellence goal.

Part III – Financial Results, Position, Condition and Auditors' Reports. In this section, TTB presents audited balance sheets, statements of net cost, changes in net position, budgetary resources, and custodial activity as of and for the years ending September 30, 2013, and September 30, 2012, and the Independent Auditors' Report on these financial statements. Also included is a report on the Bureau's internal control over financial reporting and a report on TTB's compliance with laws and regulations.

This report section also includes a discussion of budget activities for each of the Bureau's seven major programs and supplemental information, such as a history of federal excise tax collections for the past decade.

Part IV – Appendices. This section includes a list of TTB's principal officers, an organization chart, and strategic plan information that demonstrates the relationship between TTB's plan and the overall Department of the Treasury's mission and goals.

Message from the Administrator

The past year was fraught with challenges that required creative thinking and difficult decisions on the part of all government agencies. These challenges were particularly acute for TTB, a small, innovative organization that has maintained a lean business model since it was established in January 2003. This already efficient model, which has enabled us to invest the majority of our budget in core mission work, limited our options in responding to the steep, immediate funding cuts of the sequester that took effect midway through the fiscal year. As a result, services that our industry members rely on, including alcohol beverage formula and label approvals, slowed dramatically over the course of the year. Many burgeoning businesses faced a six-month wait before they could legally operate and turn a profit. These results are antithetical to the role we play in facilitating a thriving, lawful, and competitive marketplace for the industries that we regulate.

In the face of these challenges, TTB has taken a broader view, recognizing that trimming overhead and halting hiring are stopgap measures that cannot sustain the Bureau over the long term. Throughout FY 2013, we continued to make strategic changes to our programs that will help us improve our efficiency without compromising short-term mission results. In both our tax administration and trade facilitation roles, we have sought to leverage data to inform decisions, direct enforcement resources based on areas of risk, and apply technology to gain efficiencies for ourselves and for our industry members. These changes are critical to our ability to provide needed services to a growing industry and to ensure the collection of the $23 billion in annual revenues that result from their businesses.

In the labeling program, we revised our policies to shift some of the responsibility for compliant labels to alcohol beverage producers and importers. Certain label information poses a low risk to consumer health and safety and, in these areas, we effectively stepped out of the way and now allow industry members to make certain revisions to their product labels without reapplying to TTB for a new Certificate of Label Approval. These changes are a precursor to larger reforms planned for the next several years that will bring federal regulations and policies in line with modern industry practices and market realities. TTB continues to evaluate both its labeling and formulation requirements and intends to proceed with enhanced guidance and rulemaking, as appropriate, to reduce the regulatory burden for industry and to facilitate TTB's transition to market-based enforcement of these regulations.

We also continue to hone our tax enforcement strategy to deter and address fraud and other criminal activity in the alcohol and tobacco industries. Because diversion schemes vary widely, and evolve rapidly in response to enforcement efforts, we use real-time data and advanced analytics to remain flexible and responsive to revenue threats. In FY 2013, we continued to focus our enforcement efforts on the import and export trade of alcohol and tobacco, as this is a vulnerable point in the supply chain that is exploited by criminal enterprises to evade federal excise taxes. The civil and criminal cases brought to date indicate that the federal government is losing millions in revenue annually due to illicit alcohol and tobacco trade, and TTB will continue to work with its law enforcement partners to prevent criminal actors from profiting at the expense of governments and legitimate businesses.

Ensuring vibrant and compliant global trade requires that we engage and collaborate with scientific and regulatory agencies around the world. In FY 2013, TTB scientists contributed to advancements in tobacco science through the validation of new tobacco testing techniques, providing a reliable international standard for tobacco regulators to authenticate and classify certain tobacco products. TTB also opens opportunities for U.S. businesses in overseas markets, with the global trade in alcohol beverages valued at well over $3 billion. The Bureau expanded its global network of alcohol and tobacco regulators in FY 2013 by signing a memorandum of understanding with Wine Australia, an important strategic partner in promoting wine trade. We also continued to engage with economies in the Asia-Pacific rim that represent emerging markets for U.S. producers. This work ensures that markets remain open for opportunities for domestic businesses and that illegal activity in international trade is addressed promptly.

In the pages that follow, we more fully describe the year's accomplishments and discuss areas where we fell short of our desired performance. The cumulative impact of the sequester and other recent budget reductions is apparent; however, we remain undeterred in our continued resolution to more effectively and efficiently fulfill our mandates.

The Bureau has validated the accuracy, completeness, and reliability of the performance data contained in this report.

John J. Manfreda

Administrator

Vision, Mission, and Values

Vision

Our vision is to be the world's authority in the regulation, taxation, and science of alcohol and tobacco products and a model for next generation government.

Mission

Our mission is to collect the taxes on alcohol, tobacco, firearms and ammunition; protect the consumer by ensuring the integrity of alcohol products; and prevent unfair and unlawful market activity for alcohol and tobacco products.

Values

We value:

- **People.** We empower our people through trust, respect, and teamwork.

- **Results.** We take pride in accomplishing meaningful results for the American public.

- **Accessibility.** We are available to the public and our colleagues through collaboration, communication, and partnership.

- **Innovation.** We explore new and better methods of conducting business, take manageable risks to improve our operations, and evolve based on results.

- **Service.** We are professionals dedicated to public service.

TTB Strategic Goals and Objectives

Strategic Goal: Collect the Revenue

Industry remits the proper federal tax on alcohol, tobacco, firearms, and ammunition products

Tax Verification and Validation. Assure voluntary compliance in the timely and accurate remittance of tax payments

Civil and Criminal Enforcement. Detect and address excise tax evasion and other criminal violations of the Internal Revenue Code in the industries TTB regulates

Strategic Goal: Protect the Public

Alcohol and tobacco industry operators meet permit qualifications, and alcohol beverage products comply with federal production, labeling, and marketing requirements

Business Integrity. Assure that only qualified persons and business entities operate within the industries TTB regulates

Product Integrity. Assure that alcohol beverage products comply with federal production, labeling, and advertising requirements

Market Integrity. Assure fair trade practices throughout the alcohol beverage marketplace

Strategic Goal: Management and Organizational Excellence

Effectively managed resources and human capital for maximum performance, efficiency, and program results

Human Capital Management. Maintain a qualified, engaged, and satisfied workforce

Technology Solutions. Deliver effective, streamlined, and flexible IT solutions that add value and support program performance

Finance and Performance Results. Facilitate strategic management and financial accountability through the delivery of timely and reliable financial and performance information

TTB Office Locations

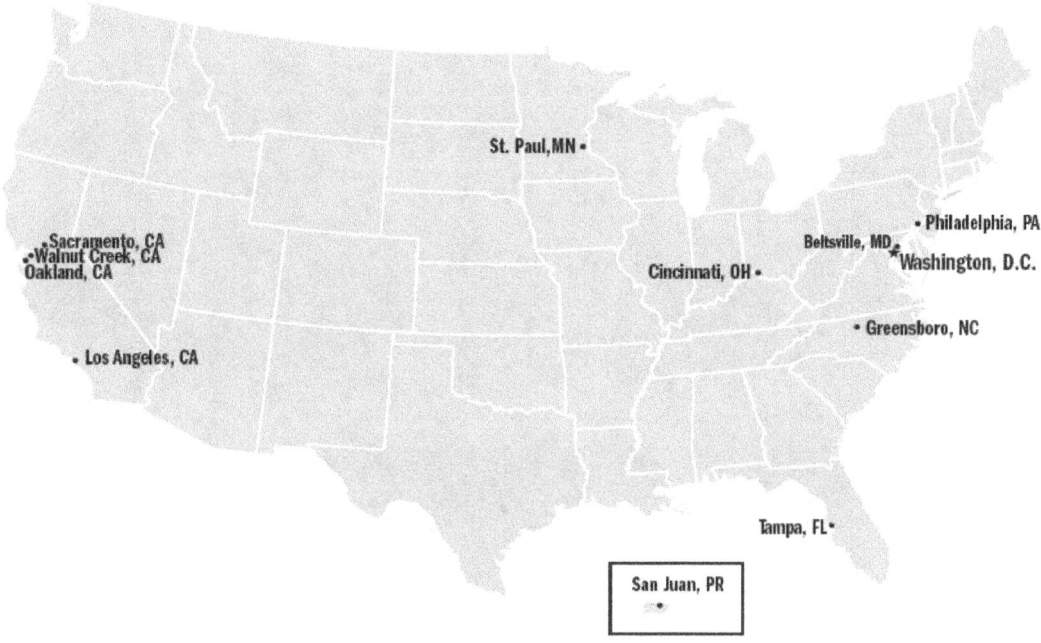

Industry at a Glance	FY 2013	FY 2012
Total TTB Permittees	66,642	61,684
TTB Permittees by Industry Type		
Alcohol	96.9%	96.7%
Tobacco	1.4%	1.5%
Firearms	1.7%	1.8%
TTB Permittees Not Subject to Tax	51,167	48,046
TTB Permittees Subject to Tax	15,475	13,643
TTB Permittees Who Filed and Paid Taxes	9,298	8,533

TTB at a Glance	2013	2012
Employees	482	496
Office Locations *	12	12
Budget Authority	$94.7 Million	$99.9 Million
Revenue Collected	$22.9 Billion	$23.4 Billion
Original and Amended Permits Processed	25,646	27,272
Certificate of Label Applications Received	140,324	152,741

*TTB has some offices co-located in larger cities.

**TTB included the Westlake, OH office on the FY 2012 map in error.

Page left intentionally blank.

Part I: Management's Discussion and Analysis

Profile of a Bureau

The mission of the Alcohol and Tobacco Tax and Trade Bureau (TTB) is to collect the federal taxes on alcohol, tobacco, firearms, and ammunition products, protect consumers from unsafe or improperly labeled alcohol beverage products, and prevent unfair or unlawful trade of alcohol and tobacco products. TTB's diverse mission, and its position as a bureau of the Department of the Treasury, means that TTB must strike a balance between its tax and regulatory functions and its role in facilitating fair and robust economic activity in the alcohol and tobacco trades.

TTB is staffed with approximately 500 employees, most of whom report to either the headquarters office in Washington, D.C., or the National Revenue Center in Cincinnati, Ohio. For its auditors, investigators, and agents to most effectively operate in the field, TTB maintains a minimal physical footprint, with 10 offices in cities across the United States and Puerto Rico. These small, strategically located offices place the Bureau in close proximity to centers of trade and industry activity, and provide effective launch points for TTB's investigative teams. Additionally, the Bureau has two laboratory facilities in Walnut Creek, California and Beltsville, Maryland. See Part IV of this report for a chart outlining the TTB organizational structure.

The Bureau was formed in January 2003, under the Homeland Security Act of 2002, but its history began more than 200 years ago as one of the earliest federal tax collection agencies. Today, TTB operates under the authorities of the Internal Revenue Code of 1986 (IRC)[1] and the Federal Alcohol Administration Act (FAA Act),[2] including the Alcoholic Beverage Labeling Act of 1988 (ABLA)[3] and the Webb-Kenyon Act.[4] These laws put in place strict requirements and controls related to alcohol and tobacco products and place restrictions on who can make, sell, and distribute these commodities.

In essence, TTB administers its jurisdiction according to two core mission areas—"Collect the Revenue" and "Protect the Public"—both of which serve to support the Nation's economic recovery by ensuring that the federal government has the cash resources needed to fund the Nation's priorities and that lawful U.S. businesses are competitive and thriving in the global marketplace.

---

1 Chapters 51 and 52 of the IRC provide for excise taxation and authorize operations of alcohol and tobacco producers and related industries, and IRC sections 4181 and 4182 provide for excise taxes for firearms and ammunition.

2 The FAA Act provides for regulation of those engaged in the alcohol beverage industry and for protection of consumers through certain requirements regarding the labeling and advertising of alcohol beverages. The FAA Act also includes provisions to preclude unfair trade practices that serve as barriers to competition and trade in the U.S. marketplace.

3 The ABLA mandates that a Government warning statement appear on all alcohol beverages offered for sale or distribution in the United States.

4 The Webb-Kenyon Act prohibits the shipment of alcohol beverages into a State in violation of the receiving state's laws.

Alcohol Industry Snapshot

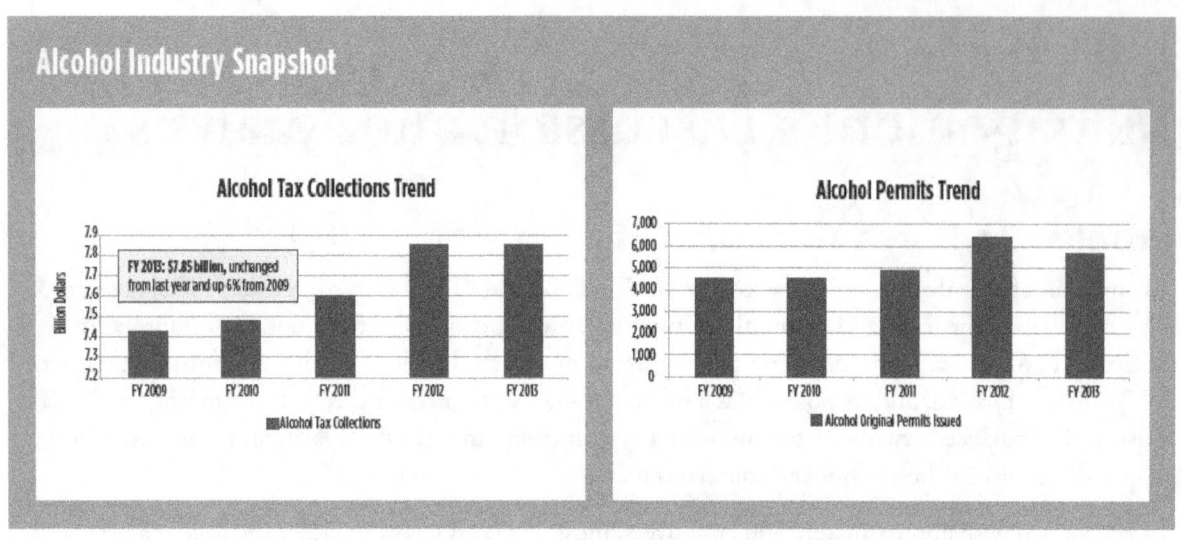

Alcohol Tax Collections Trend

FY 2013: $7.85 billion, unchanged from last year and up 6% from 2009

■ Alcohol Tax Collections

Alcohol Permits Trend

■ Alcohol Original Permits Issued

Tobacco Industry Snapshot

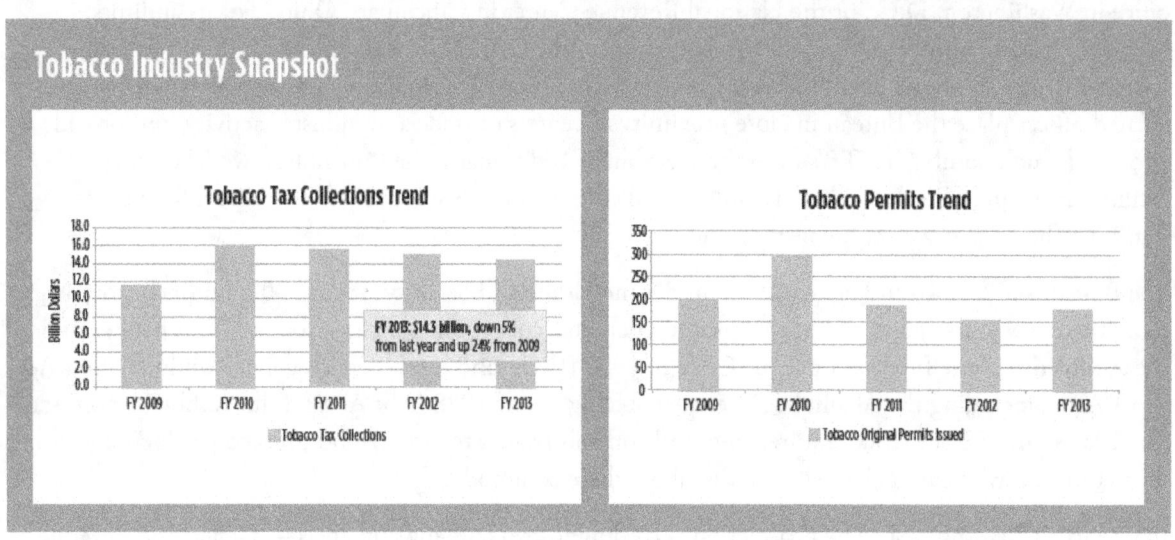

Tobacco Tax Collections Trend

FY 2013: $14.3 billion, down 5% from last year and up 24% from 2009

■ Tobacco Tax Collections

Tobacco Permits Trend

■ Tobacco Original Permits Issued

Firearms & Ammunition Industry Snapshot

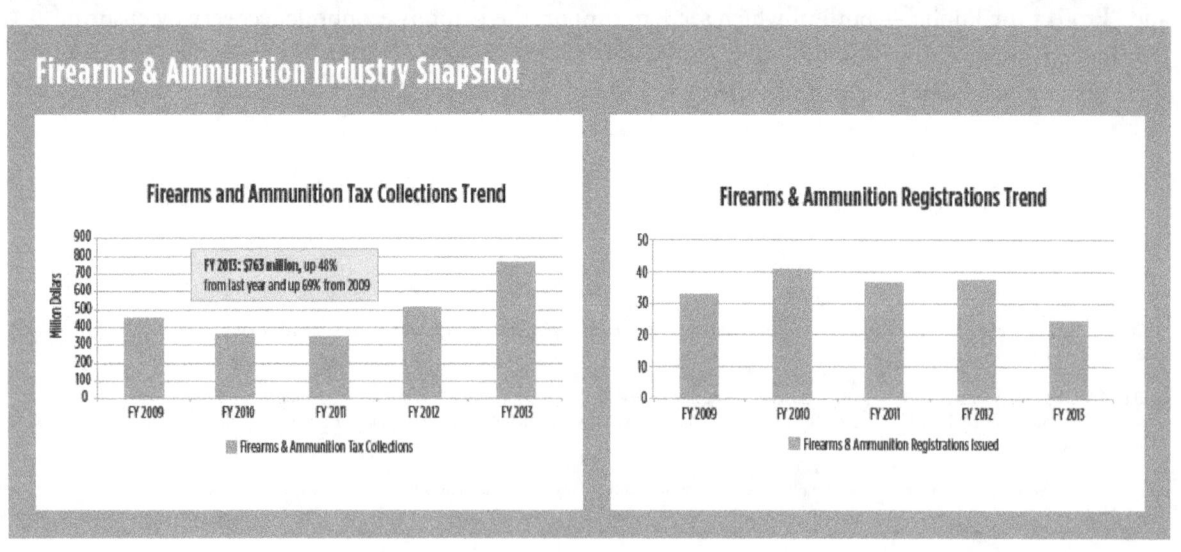

Firearms and Ammunition Tax Collections Trend

FY 2013: $763 million, up 48% from last year and up 69% from 2009

■ Firearms & Ammunition Tax Collections

Firearms & Ammunition Registrations Trend

■ Firearms 8 Ammunition Registrations Issued

Collect the Revenue

TTB is the third largest tax collection agency in the U.S. government, behind the Internal Revenue Service (IRS) and U.S. Customs and Border Protection (CBP). Annual revenues from the alcohol, tobacco, firearms, and ammunition industries are approximately $23 billion. TTB excise tax collections reached an historic high of $23.8 billion in FY 2010, principally due to increased receipts from the tobacco industry. Today, tobacco revenues comprise more than 60 percent of TTB's total excise tax collections.

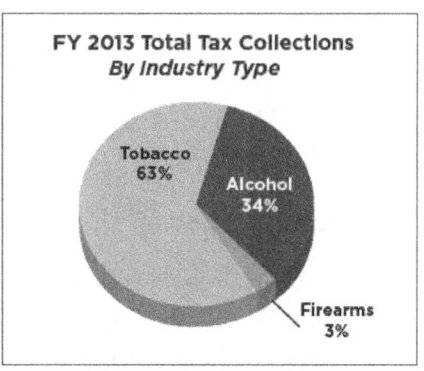

FY 2013 Total Tax Collections By Industry Type

Tobacco 63%
Alcohol 34%
Firearms 3%

In FY 2013, TTB collected $14.3 billion in tobacco tax revenue, a decrease of approximately 5 percent compared to FY 2012 collections. In forecasting tobacco revenue, the Congressional Budget Office (CBO) predicted that federal collections would decline after peaking in FY 2010 due to the significantly increased tax rates on cigarettes and other tobacco products enacted by the Children's Health Insurance Program Reauthorization Act (CHIPRA). This legislation provided for a tax increase on all tobacco products (except large cigars), cigarette papers, and cigarette tubes, effective April 1, 2009. Higher prices on tobacco products have historically resulted in decreased consumption and increased illicit trade, which indicates that tobacco revenue will continue to decline. Further, recent analysis of tobacco collections has shown significant market shifts for tobacco products since the passage of CHIPRA. The law introduced large federal excise tax disparities among tobacco products, which created opportunities for tax avoidance and led manufacturers and price sensitive consumers to shift toward lower-taxed products. TTB's efforts in enforcing both its civil and criminal tax jurisdiction support voluntary tax compliance and act to deter illicit trade, and TTB will continue to act to address the revenue threat posed by the diversion of alcohol and tobacco products to ensure the collection of the taxes due.

The alcohol beverage industry in the United States accounts for approximately 30 percent of the excise tax revenue collected by TTB. In FY 2013, TTB collected approximately $7.9 billion in revenue from U.S. wineries, breweries, and distilleries, down slightly compared to the prior year. While economic forecasts predict continued modest growth in the U.S. alcohol industry as a whole, excise tax collections will likely remain relatively flat due to a number of variables, including increasing volumes in imports and exports, and declining sales by volume from the country's largest breweries, which account for over 90 percent of the beer sold in the U.S. The rapid expansion of new small alcohol beverage producers, including small wineries and "craft" breweries and distilleries, will not entirely offset the declines in sales and tax payments by the large companies because these producers have lower production volumes and small beer and wine producers are eligible for reduced tax rates based on their production volume. This trend is expected to continue into FY 2015.

TTB also collects the federal excise taxes on firearms and ammunition. These taxes are remitted to the Fish and Wildlife Restoration Fund. This trust fund was established by statute and is overseen by the U.S. Fish and Wildlife Service, which apportions the money to state governments for wildlife restoration and research and hunter education programs. In the past decade, collections have increased from $193 million in FY 2003 to an estimated $763 million in FY 2013, an increase of $570 million over the past decade, or a 295 percent growth in tax revenue. Significant revenue shifts occurred between fiscal years 2011 and 2013, with collections increasing nearly 50 percent year-to-year. Historically, the increase in reported tax revenue can be attributed to external factors, such as increased sales, as well as TTB's enforcement presence, which increases collections and promotes voluntary compliance.

Civil Tax Enforcement

Tax Classification

The tax rate on alcohol and tobacco products depends on a variety of factors, including product type (i.e., wine, spirits, or malt beverage) as well as characteristics of the products themselves, such as composition and weight. A critical first step in tax enforcement is the assignment of a tax class to alcohol and tobacco products based on federal regulatory standards.

For alcohol beverages, classification requires that TTB review the formula of certain products before they enter the market. For example, if an examination of the formula reveals that an imported sake, which is made from fermented rice and is classified and taxed as wine, contains added spirits, then the product is then classified and taxed as a distilled spirits product. This type of formula review, known as a pre-import approval, can have significant tax implications, as wine is subject to a lower tax rate than spirits products.

TTB also conducts marketplace product evaluations to check for proper tax classification based on the characteristics of the product as defined by statute. As an example, TTB evaluates samples of products marketed as large cigars to verify that the products are large cigars rather than cigarettes or small cigars, as the tax rates differ markedly between these products. In classifying such a product for tax purposes, TTB evaluates the product's wrapper, the type of tobacco used in the filler, the product's packaging and labeling, and its weight to verify that the product meets the statutory criteria for a large cigar.

Shifting Market Trends due to Tax Rates

The increase in the federal excise tax rate on cigarettes and other tobacco products highlights the importance of TTB's tax classification activities. Prior to CHIPRA, TTB faced enforcement challenges due to the disparate tax rates on cigarettes and small cigars, and challenges in applying the statutory criteria to these products. The law resolved a longstanding tax enforcement challenge for TTB by creating parity in the excise tax rates for cigarettes and small cigars. However, CHIPRA created large disparities in tax rates for other tobacco products, thus presenting new challenges for TTB in appropriately classifying and collecting the taxes due on these products based on their substantial similarities. Since the new tax rates took effect in April 2009, TTB has identified and monitored significant market shifts toward lower-taxed tobacco products by manufacturers and price-sensitive consumers.

In the past five years, TTB data indicates a near complete reversal in the market share for pipe and roll-your-own (RYO) tobacco in response to the lower tax rate on pipe tobacco.[5] Similarly, the market share for small cigars and large cigars, which was relatively equal pre-CHIPRA, has starkly shifted toward large cigars as these products are subject to an ad valorum tax and can have significantly lower tax rates depending on the sale price of the cigar.[6]

Because of the lack of clear standards in the tax code to differentiate pipe tobacco from RYO tobacco, and the consequent potential for misclassification and erroneous tax payment on these products, TTB has initiated rulemaking on the types of objective standards that would provide a basis for differentiating between these two products for tax purposes. At the same time, the TTB Tobacco Laboratory has been evaluating proposed methods and standards, and undertaking research to develop additional methods and standards, in support of this rulemaking. The goal is to set forth objective criteria, based on physical characteristics of the products, to distinguish between pipe tobacco and RYO for tax purposes. TTB intends to publish subsequent rulemaking in this area.

Market Shifts in Tobacco Products

Significant shifts in the tobacco products industry have developed since the enactment of CHIPRA, particularly for small and large cigars and RYO and pipe tobacco. An independent review by the Government Accountability Office (GAO) examined the market shifts in smoking tobacco products since CHIPRA, examined the impact of those market shifts on federal revenue, and evaluated TTB's actions to respond. In its 2012 report (GAO-12-475) on shifts in tobacco product removals since the tobacco tax rate increase, GAO estimates that federal revenue losses due to market shifts from RYO to pipe tobacco and from small to large cigars could exceed $1.1 billion for the period April 2009 through September 2011. GAO recommended that Congress consider equalizing tax rates on RYO and pipe tobacco and, in consultation with the Department of the Treasury, consider options for reducing tax avoidance due to tax differentials between small and large cigars. GAO also recognized that TTB has taken steps to respond to these market shifts, including its efforts to differentiate between RYO and pipe tobacco for tax collection purposes, but acknowledged that TTB has limited options. Current data indicates that this trend continued in FY 2013.

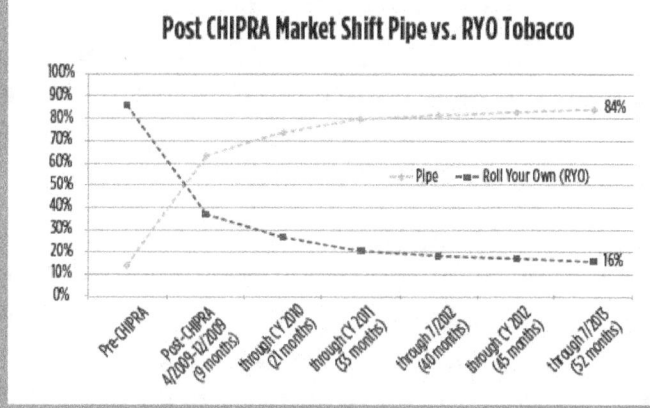

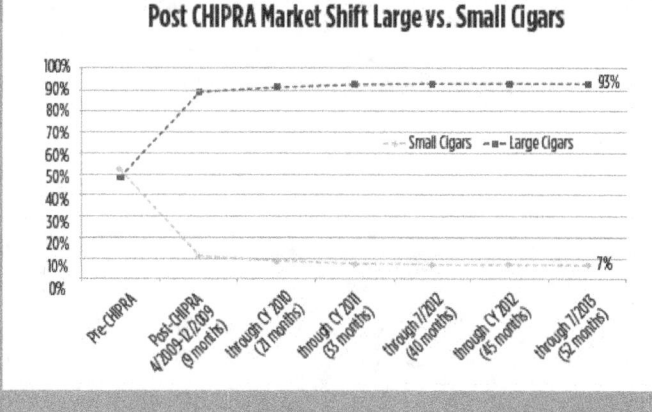

---

5 Prior to CHIPRA, the tax rates on pipe tobacco and RYO tobacco were the same at just under $1.10 per pound. As a result of CHIPRA, the tax on pipe tobacco was increased to just over $2.83 per pound, while the tax on RYO tobacco was increased to $24.78 per pound.

6 Large cigars are the only tobacco product for which the excise tax is based on the manufacturer or importer's sale price; all other tobacco products are taxed at a flat rate based either on the number of units or the weight of the product. The *ad valorum* tax on large cigars can result in significantly lower tax rates on these products, depending on the sale price of the cigar. As a result, since the tax increase on small cigars, TTB has found that manufacturers and importers are increasing the weight of products that TTB had previously evaluated and determined to be small cigars prior to CHIPRA so that they meet the statutory definition of a large cigar.

Supporting Global Tax Administration by Advancing Tobacco Science

As an international authority on the technical analysis of alcohol and tobacco products, TTB's expertise is sought after by domestic partners and foreign counterparts to support an effective global excise tax enforcement scheme. TTB also actively pursues opportunities for collaboration to support its tax and regulatory mission.

TTB's Tobacco Laboratory is a government leader in the development of methods and protocols to identify physical characteristics of tobacco products for regulatory and tax enforcement purposes. In FY 2013, TTB's Tobacco Laboratory developed a method for humectant analysis in various tobacco products. Industry adds humectants to tobacco products to retain moisture content and extend a product's shelf life. The TTB Tobacco Laboratory has analyzed humectants in pipe tobacco and RYO tobacco in support of future rulemaking to distinguish these products because humectant concentration is a physical characteristic that may provide an objective standard to support tax classification determinations. TTB also participated in an international collaboration study to validate the humectant analysis methods proposed by the World Health Organization (WHO) and the Tobacco Laboratory Network (TobLabNet), a global tobacco testing laboratory network. This effort supports the identification and acceptance of an internationally recognized consensus method for the analysis of humectants in tobacco products.

TTB also published a paper in the *Journal of Agriculture and Food Chemistry* comparing two accepted methods used by TTB and the tobacco industry to analyze carbohydrates in tobacco products. As major components of tobacco products, carbohydrates are valuable for product characterization and support TTB's efforts to develop objective criteria to determine the tax class of tobacco products. Based on TTB's findings, industry members may use either technique for analysis of raw and processed tobacco without concern that the other method will generate different results.

In FY 2013, TTB organized the second meeting of the North American Tobacco Regulatory Laboratory Network technical forum, which met in September 2013 at the TTB

National Laboratory Center in Beltsville, Maryland. Thirty-five scientists and regulators representing 11 federal agencies from the United States, Canada, and Mexico participated in the forum to discuss tobacco science in the context of tobacco regulation. TTB established the forum to foster the exchange of information on technical regulatory matters and collaboration on testing protocols and analytical methods to proactively address emerging issues on tobacco. Forum participants identified tobacco leaves and tobacco flavor projects as major areas for collaboration and formed working groups to begin enhancing technical capabilities.

In the alcohol field, TTB developed a new capability using isotope ratios to determine the difference between naturally sparkling wines and wines that are artificially carbonated. This capability is important because naturally sparkling wines and artificially carbonated wines fall into different tax classes, and producers may label artificially carbonated wines as naturally sparkling wines to evade federal taxes and defraud consumers. TTB participated in an international study with laboratories from France, Germany, Brazil, and Uruguay to validate this capability, with TTB's results comparing favorably to the international group's results. The participating laboratories are discussing future studies to support tax classification and address other fraudulently labeled alcohol products.

In FY 2013, TTB also coordinated an international wine technical forum, which provided an opportunity for TTB to address emerging technical issues and encourage scientific collaboration between TTB, industry scientists, and other wine regulators. Participants at this year's forum included representatives from TTB, the Wine Institute, the Unione Italiani Vini (an Italian wine trade organization), the World Wine Trade Group, and the Asia-Pacific Economic Cooperation (APEC). The technical principles discussed during the international forum focused on establishing regulatory limits for wine and testing wine for compliance. These technical principles will serve as the foundation for a multi-year project to promote coherence in wine regulation throughout the APEC region.

Addressing Revenue Threat from Roll-Your-Own Cigarette Machines

The current tax differential on certain tobacco products has also contributed to the proliferation of cigarette manufacturing machines at retail establishments and other venues for consumer use. Following the enactment of CHIPRA, TTB began receiving reports of retail establishments maintaining commercial cigarette-making machines on their premises for customers to use in the manufacture of cigarettes. TTB received reports that customers were purchasing pipe tobacco for RYO to avoid the higher excise tax rate on RYO, and then used the cigarette-making machines to produce lower cost cigarettes using pipe tobacco.

In July 2012, Congress enacted the Moving Ahead for Progress in the 21st Century Act (H.R. 4348, also known as "MAP-21"), which definitively addressed the legal status of retailers that provide cigarette-making machines to customers. The law clarified that any person who for commercial purposes makes available for consumer use a machine capable of making tobacco products (including cigarettes) is a manufacturer of tobacco products. TTB issued public guidance in October 2012 to clarify that these manufacturers must comply with all applicable statutory and regulatory requirements, including applying for a permit from TTB and paying federal excise taxes. The guidance also clarified that non-profit organizations, social clubs, cooperatives, and other similar organizations that made RYO machines available to members were not exempt from these requirements. In early FY 2013, TTB initiated enforcement actions on approximately 1,300 locations suspected of illegally operating RYO cigarette machines. To date, this enforcement initiative has resulted in the identification of approximately $1 million in tax liabilities and the initiation of several criminal investigations.

Tax Verification

In effecting its revenue mission, TTB uses a strategic risk-based approach to verify that industry members remit the excise taxes due on the alcohol, tobacco, firearms, and ammunition products sold to U.S. consumers. This strategy enables TTB to cover a wide universe of taxpayers and establish an identifiable enforcement presence to deter industry members and others from engaging in diversion activity. This involves a combination of risk modeling and data analytics to support the identification of the highest risk activity for audit or investigation. Continuous refinements to these models and sound intelligence enable TTB to efficiently deploy its limited enforcement resources to address the most serious revenue threats.

TTB also relies on a coordinated enforcement approach in verifying proper tax payment. The Bureau's auditors, investigators, agents, and intelligence analysts all contribute critical skills to detecting and addressing tax evasion. Due to the complexity of diversion schemes, these skills are often combined in the form of National Response Teams that identify and investigate major diversion cases with potential nationwide impact, helping to ensure the successful prosecution of offenders. TTB also applies advanced investigative techniques to detect diversion, which include the tracing of products through the supply chain to the point of diversion. Combined, these efforts resulted in civil and criminal cases and the identification of approximately $18 million in excise tax liability in FY 2013 alone. Further, TTB's forward trace investigations have identified an underground market for whole leaf tobacco used to manufacture "blunt" wrappers used to smoke marijuana, indicating a relationship between marijuana and taxable tobacco products that warrants further evaluation. Though the whole leaf tobacco itself is unregulated and untaxed, cutting the leaf to manufacture blunt wrappers requires a permit and is subject to federal excise tax.

Enforcing Compliance in the Import and Export Trade

Due to the known revenue risk in the import and export trade in alcohol and tobacco products, in FY 2013, TTB continued to focus its enforcement on these at-risk points in the supply chain. TTB's efforts, in collaboration with CBP, have ensured an even playing field in the international trade of alcohol and tobacco.

As the federal permitting authority for alcohol and tobacco importers, TTB developed risk models to identify high-risk activity and importers. In FY 2013, TTB continued to enhance and test its risk models with the goal of allowing for more real-time identification of high-risk activity for enforcement action. To date, this initiative has resulted in the identification of more than $11.5 million in additional excise tax liability associated with imported alcohol and tobacco products. TTB has referred these cases to CBP, the agency responsible for collecting the federal excise tax on imported products.

TTB extends its enforcement reach through interagency cooperative efforts. In particular, TTB is partnering with CBP's Office of Regulatory Audits (ORA) to ensure that the taxes due on imported products are collected. In FY 2013, TTB and CBP's ORA conducted a joint audit of a tobacco importer. This pilot effort resulted in the identification of $6.3 million in federal excise taxes, and TTB is working with CBP on collection. Additionally, TTB and CBP jointly developed and implemented new protocols for tax collections on TTB-regulated commodities to strengthen federal tax enforcement.

Exports also pose a significant revenue threat because alcohol and tobacco products intended for export may be placed in a customs bonded warehouse, foreign trade zone, or tobacco export warehouse without payment of tax because they are not intended for the U.S. market. Some tax evasion schemes involve diversion of these products into domestic commerce to evade federal excise taxes. According to TTB data, non-taxpaid removals of alcohol and tobacco products from bonded premises have an annual excise tax exposure of about $380 million and $1 billion, respectively. In FY 2013, TTB auditors and investigators, as well as five National Response Teams, examined suspected tax fraud and diversion at export warehouses. Though these investigations are time intensive, and often require forward trace investigations, the results to date indicate significant diversion activity. Based on these investigations, TTB has initiated more than $3 million in tax assessments and anticipates taking actions on the permits of the implicated companies. Going forward, TTB intends to expand its proven intelligence and investigative techniques to make significant inroads into identifying tax evasion schemes that involve the diversion of non-taxpaid products intended for export.

Addressing the Revenue Risk from Tobacco Processors

Manufacturers and importers of processed tobacco distribute roughly 1.1 billion pounds of processed tobacco annually to a myriad of brokers, manufacturers, and other tobacco processors for use in cigarettes and other taxable tobacco products. Manufacturers and importers of processed tobacco must obtain a TTB permit and report to TTB on the first removal, transfer, or sale of processed tobacco. As processed tobacco is untaxed, the diversion of this product outside the lawful distribution chain for use in the illegal manufacture of cigarettes or other tobacco products poses a significant revenue risk. As a result, limited reporting requirements and the unrestricted sale of processed tobacco create additional enforcement challenges in detecting and addressing tobacco diversion.

During FY 2012, TTB developed a risk model to detect high-risk removals and sales of processed tobacco, and used a combination of audits and forward trace investigations to determine if the product was used in the illicit manufacturing of tobacco products. In FY 2013, TTB continued to address this identified revenue threat and, to date, TTB's investigations into this area have resulted in multiple civil and criminal cases that have identified more than $180 million in potential revenue loss from the diversion of more than 10 million pounds of processed tobacco to non-permitted entities.

Criminal Enforcement

TTB is the federal agency responsible for detecting and addressing federal excise tax evasion in relation to alcohol and tobacco products. Under its criminal authority, TTB is charged with identifying any gaps in tax payment from entities and individuals manufacturing or selling alcohol and tobacco products outside of the lawful distribution system. The diversion of these products outside of legitimate commercial channels without the payment of taxes due threatens federal revenues, undermines fair competition, and provides a well-established source of funding for criminal enterprises.

Accurately measuring the loss in federal tax receipts from alcohol and tobacco diversion is difficult because of the clandestine nature of the activity.[7] However, in any case where the intrinsic value of a product is dwarfed by its tax value, there is incentive to evade the tax to gain an illegal profit. In its 2009 review of

---

7 In February 2010, the Department of the Treasury issued a report to Congress ("Report to Congress on Federal Tax Receipts Lost Due to Illicit Trade and Recommendations for Increased Enforcement"), which included an effort to estimate the amount of Federal tax receipts lost as a result of cigarette diversion. The study emphasized the substantial uncertainty surrounding the magnitude of the Federal tax receipts lost due to cigarette diversion.

federal tobacco tax enforcement efforts, the Department of Justice Office of the Inspector General cited federal and state government estimates of $5 billion in annual revenue losses resulting from the diversion of tobacco products.[8]

Recent increases in federal and state tobacco tax rates have further increased the profit incentive to engage in cigarette trafficking, which has resulted in a proliferation of tobacco diversion schemes. A March 2011 Government Accountability Office Report found that there are a wide range of schemes used to evade tobacco excise taxes and fees and described the scope of current diversion activity, which extends to high and low tax states alike, as well as to Native American lands and other countries.[9] However, the diversion of products to evade federal excise tax is not limited to tobacco. Though TTB has no similar estimates of revenue losses from the diversion of alcohol, TTB's criminal cases indicate that fraud in the alcohol beverage trade poses both a public safety risk and a serious revenue threat.

Using temporary appropriations, TTB has developed an effective criminal enforcement program by leveraging existing law enforcement agents within the Treasury Department to enforce its criminal jurisdiction. This arrangement has allowed TTB to engage in operations quickly and bypass certain operational costs, both of which are critical considerations given continued funding uncertainties. TTB uses forensic auditing and advanced investigative techniques to respond to constantly evolving diversion schemes, which vary widely and change in response to targeted enforcement efforts. TTB's techniques have proven effective in narrowing the tax gap in the tobacco and alcohol industries and contributing to deficit reduction through additional revenue collections.

Achieving Criminal Enforcement Results

In three years of operations, the TTB criminal enforcement program has produced significant results, particularly given the early stage of the program. Using a small contingent of agents supported by a robust team of auditors, investigators, and intelligence analysts, TTB has opened a total of 64 cases, 18 of which were opened in FY 2013. In total, TTB's criminal cases have identified nearly $350 million in estimated tax liability from the diversion of alcohol and tobacco products, with one ongoing case initiated in FY 2103 involving over $150 million in tax liabilities. To date, TTB's special agents have participated in criminal seizures valued at approximately $117 million based upon violations under TTB's jurisdiction.

TTB has worked jointly with local, state, and other federal agencies, including the IRS, CBP, FDA, ATF, and Homeland Security Investigations, to investigate and develop criminal cases under TTB's jurisdiction. Coordinating with other law enforcement partners leads to stronger cases and ensures a unified federal enforcement presence to deter future criminal activity. Based on charges outside of TTB's primary jurisdiction, including money laundering and Contraband Cigarette Trafficking Act violations, TTB has identified an additional $2.7 million in revenue due to the government.

---

8 "The Bureau of Alcohol, Tobacco, Firearms and Explosives' Efforts to Prevent Diversion of Tobacco," U.S. Department of Justice, Office of the Inspector General, Report No. I-2009-005, Sept. 2009.

9 "Illicit Tobacco: Various Schemes are Used to Evade Taxes and Fees," U.S. Government Accountability Office, GAO-11-313, March 2011.

TTB has identified criminal activity across the industries it regulates, with approximately 61 percent of its initiated diversion cases related to tobacco products, 33 percent related to alcohol beverage products, 5 percent involving alcohol and tobacco products, and 1 percent related to evasion of the firearms and ammunition excise tax. The schemes employed to evade excise tax payment include:

- Manufacturing of tobacco products without payment of Federal excise tax

- Cigarette distributors evading tobacco floor stocks tax

- Cigarette distributors selling "exported" cigarettes in the U.S. without payment of federal excise tax

- Cigarettes smuggled into the U.S. without payment of federal excise tax

- Failure to pay federal excise tax on distilled spirits

- Importation of misclassified distilled spirits to evade federal excise tax

- Operating without a permit/wholesaling violations

- Importing alcohol without a permit

- False wine labeling and sales of counterfeit wine

In FY 2013, TTB presented 18 cases to the U.S. Attorney's Office, of which 17 have been accepted to date, for a 94 percent acceptance rate. The high acceptance rate for TTB's criminal referrals demonstrates both the merit and the magnitude of these cases. In addition, TTB maintains a 100 percent conviction rate on the TTB cases that have been resolved through the legal system. In FY 2013, the amount of tax loss at issue in the cases recommended for prosecution exceeded $57 million.

Significantly, though criminal cases are often multi-year endeavors, TTB has already resolved several cases in the three years since the launch of TTB's criminal enforcement program. In FY 2013, a defendant convicted on tobacco diversion charges was sentenced to five years of incarceration, followed by three years of supervised release, and ordered to pay restitution of $10 million and forfeit $19 million. Another defendant was sentenced to one year of incarceration and ordered to pay nearly $1 million in restitution for filing false federal excise tax returns on manufactured distilled spirits.

Protect the Public

TTB's public protection mission includes a wide range of activities that directly impact American consumers and the U.S. economy. TTB's role in regulating the trade of alcohol and tobacco products ensures not only consumer confidence in the integrity of the products manufactured in the U.S., but also that businesses are operating on a level playing field—key outcomes that promote job growth and a strong economy.

TTB's work in this mission area aligns under three main programs: 1) Permits and Business Assurance; 2) Trade Facilitation; and 3) Advertising, Labeling, and Product Safety. Taken together, these programs ensure the integrity of the businesses that produce and distribute alcohol and tobacco products, the integrity of the alcohol beverage products, and the integrity of the market in which these businesses operate.

Business Integrity

TTB facilitates growth in the U.S. economy by ensuring that only qualified applicants enter business as an alcohol producer, wholesaler, or importer, or as a tobacco products manufacturer, importer, or exporter. The FAA Act includes provisions that require a permit for alcohol beverage producers, importers, or wholesalers; the IRC includes similar permitting requirements for tobacco manufacturers, importers, and export warehouses, as well as some alcohol industry members. The number of applicants filing for an original permit or registration with TTB has grown 40 percent between fiscal years 2009 and 2013. Today, the Bureau regulates over 66,600 industry members.

Under its FAA Act authority, TTB conducts a multi-tiered background evaluation prior to issuing a permit to ensure that only qualified persons obtain a permit to operate within the TTB-regulated industries. Through this process and other activities under its Permits and Business Assurance Program, TTB prevents prohibited persons from commencing operations and potentially diverting products from legitimate commercial channels to fund illicit activity. Given the substantial tax revenue associated with the commodities TTB regulates, this activity also plays an important role in protecting federal revenues.

Efficiency in permit processing is equally critical to support improved economic opportunities for U.S. businesses. Prompt turnaround times for permit application processing enables those who are qualified to hold a federal permit to begin their operations sooner, facilitating U.S. economic growth in a fair marketplace.

Improving Service in Permit Processing

TTB processes applications for 23 types of permits or registrations for the alcohol, tobacco, firearms, and ammunition industries. New or existing alcohol and tobacco industry members must be approved by TTB in order to commence a new regulated industry operation. The new businesses permitted by TTB are predominantly small businesses, which contribute to local job opportunities as well as America's competitiveness in the global market.

Industry growth over the past several years has been striking, with the number of small producers increasing an average of between 10 – 20 percent annually. Over the same time period, TTB resources have declined, making it difficult to maintain prompt processing times. It is critical for TTB to address delays in permit issuance to avoid being in an obstructive posture at a time when job creation and United States competitiveness abroad are national priorities.

TTB completed its rollout of Permits Online, its electronic system for filing original and amended permits, in FY 2012. The impact of Permits Online has been substantial. Without this intervening action, TTB projected that average processing times would have averaged between 90 - 120 days by early FY 2012 and into FY 2013, compared to an average of 65 days just three years prior.

Alcohol Industry Members

Active Wineries and Bonded Wine Cellars

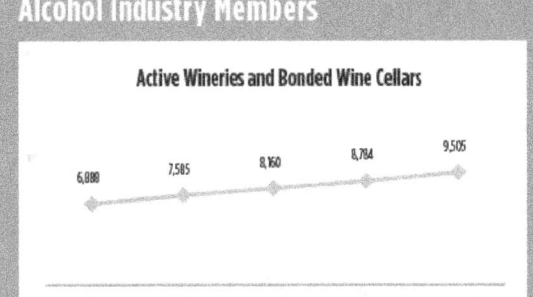

6,888   7,585   8,160   8,784   9,505

FY 2009   FY 2010   FY 2011   FY 2012   FY 2013

Active Breweries

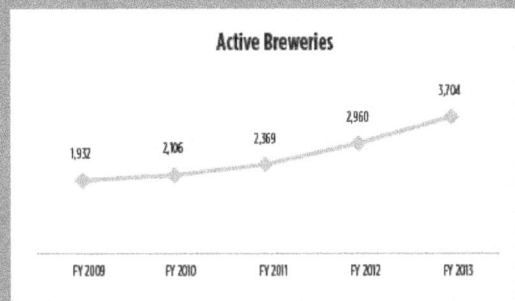

1,932   2,106   2,369   2,960   3,704

FY 2009   FY 2010   FY 2011   FY 2012   FY 2013

Active Distilleries

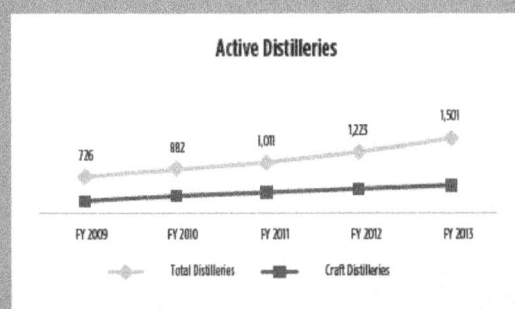

726   882   1,011   1,223   1,501

FY 2009   FY 2010   FY 2011   FY 2012   FY 2013

Total Distilleries   Craft Distilleries

The number of U.S. wineries, breweries, and distilleries continues to increase. The wine industry has grown at a relatively constant pace in each of the past five years, increasing an average of 9 percent each year. Since 2009, the number of wineries has grown nearly 40 percent.

U.S. breweries increased steadily between 2009 and 2011 and, in both 2012 and 2013, increased 25 percent over the prior year. In five years, the number of breweries has increased 98 percent. Market data indicates that growth is strong in the craft brewer segment, which includes microbreweries and brewpubs.

Since 2009, there has also been significant growth in the number of distillers, which increased by 107 percent in five years. This growth is driven by a booming craft distilling industry, defined as beverage distilled spirits producers that taxpaid less than 100,000 proof gallons annually. This segment has increased by 122 percent since 2009.

However, TTB processing times are increasing annually, largely driven by the influx of permit applications and limited staff to process them. Even as electronic filing rates reached 70 percent, the average processing times increased nearly two weeks, from 69 days in FY 2012 to 81 days in FY 2013. Although electronic processing reduces application errors as well as the time and resources needed to return incomplete applications, it does not decrease the time needed by TTB to review each application. As a result, addressing delays in application processing requires broader reforms in TTB's business processes.

In FY 2103, to curb increasing turnaround times, TTB concentrated its system enhancements on improvements to streamline the application review and approval processes. These changes addressed bottlenecks in the approval process and eliminated certain manual and paper-based processes. TTB also identified and implemented improvements to every facet of the processing workflow, from initial assignments to permit approval or denial.

TTB intends to improve processing times in FY 2014 through a combination of initiatives that involve further streamlining TTB's internal procedures, increased industry outreach, and ongoing system enhancements. TTB will also update its risk model and procedures used to process permit applications, including through adding new financial data sources and improving the risk criteria used to vet alcohol and tobacco permit applicants. Increased focus on risk modeling and statistical sampling will help TTB maintain its assurance that it is permitting only qualified applicants while managing workloads.

TTB is also taking steps to speed its transition to an entirely online processing environment. System enhancements in development for fiscal years 2014 and 2015 include the upload of historical permit application data from TTB's legacy permit and tax database to the Permits Online system. This initiative will allow the approximately 60,000 TTB permittees who originally filed a paper permit

FY 2013 Permittees by State

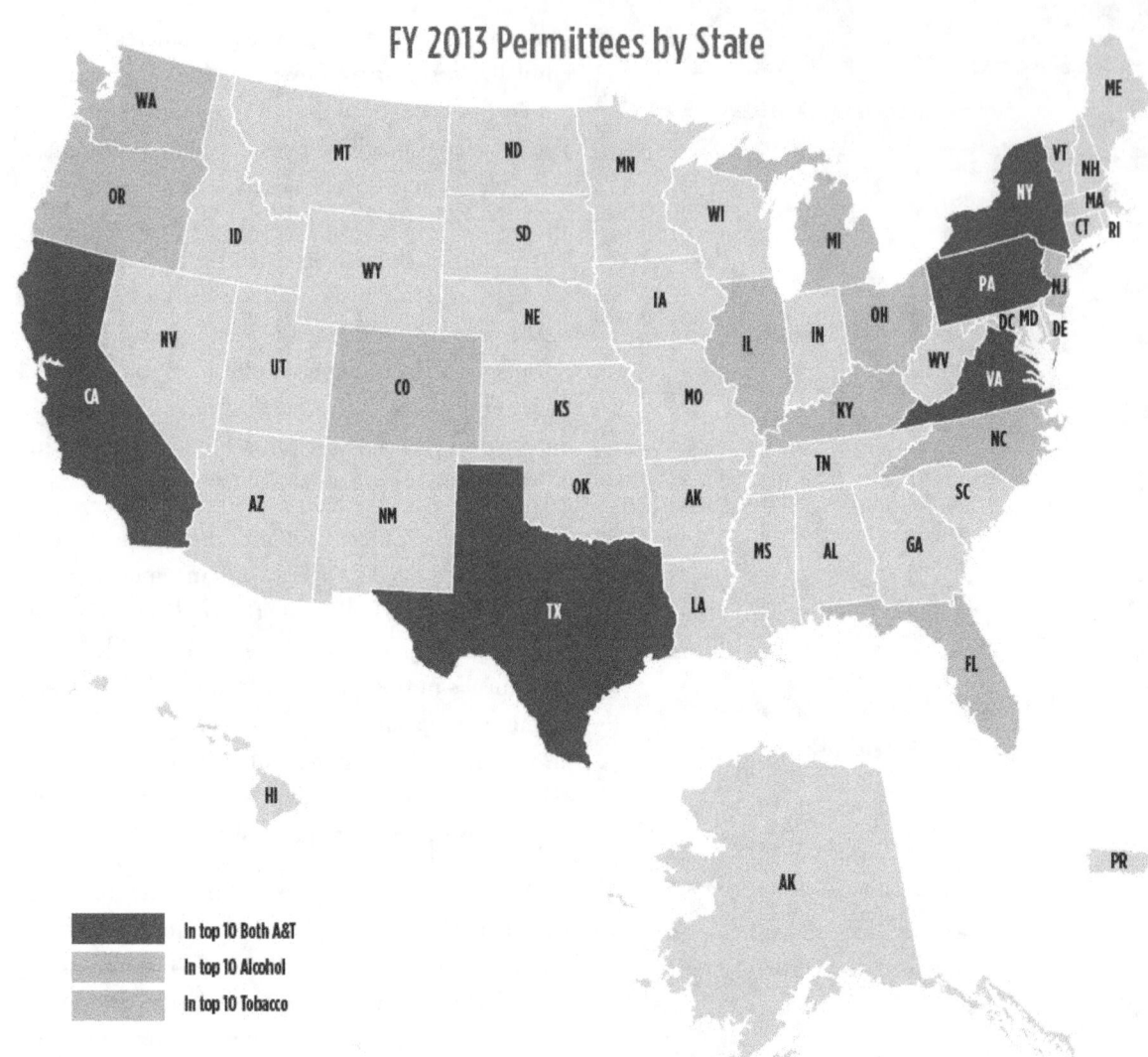

- In top 10 Both A&T
- In top 10 Alcohol
- In top 10 Tobacco

Top 10 States by Number of Alcohol Permits

State	# Active Permit Holders
California	4,273
Washington	1,265
Oregon	789
New York	684
Texas	560
Michigan	484
Pennsylvania	437
Colorado	402
Virginia	393
Ohio	370

Top 10 States by Number of Tobacco Permits

State	# Active Permit Holders
Florida	243
California	93
New York	78
North Carolina	77
Texas	45
Pennsylvania	27
Virginia	27
New Jersey	36
Kentucky	22
Illinois	21

application to electronically file for amendments to their permit (i.e., change in control or change in address) through Permits Online. As TTB receives an average of 18,000 – 20,000 permit amendments annually, this project will result in efficiencies for both TTB and the businesses it serves.

Importing Tobacco Products without a Permit

In support of the Bureau's business integrity objectives, TTB monitors compliance with federal permit requirements among tobacco product importers through a variety of data analysis and investigative techniques. In FY 2013, TTB intelligence analysts identified that 11 percent of active tobacco importers had imported products illegally during the fiscal year. TTB took appropriate enforcement action to address each instance of non-compliance. TTB's analysis of import data in FY 2013 also indicated that the vast majority of non-permitted importers are individuals purchasing tobacco products through online tobacco outlets and shipping them via the U.S. Postal Service (USPS) and FedEx. As appropriate, TTB coordinates with the USPS and other ground carriers to take enforcement action against violations within the Bureau's purview. These efforts to identify and address compliance violations have proven effective, as all of the importer entities contacted by TTB have subsequently complied with their legal obligations or ceased operations.

Further, due to TTB's enforcement efforts, the rate of non-permitted tobacco importers that have declared entries of tobacco products to U.S. Customs has declined from 22 percent to 11 percent over the past six years. As tobacco products are often smuggled into the U.S. through undeclared importations, however, TTB must continue to supplement these data mining efforts and to monitor importer activity through audits, investigations, and other intelligence efforts to detect undeclared importations and address the substantial potential tax losses that they represent.

Market Integrity

TTB is charged with ensuring that the alcohol marketplace is free from practices that would stifle competition and act as a barrier to trade. TTB meets this mandate through a variety of activities under its Trade Facilitation program, ranging from investigations of industry trade practices to engaging foreign counterpart agencies to keep the channels of commerce open and operating in compliance with U.S. and international laws.

TTB's work in this area directly influences the Nation's economic recovery. Industry trade association reports[10] state that the alcohol beverage industry contributes directly or indirectly to the U.S. economy by providing nearly 4 million jobs and roughly $400 - $500 billion in economic activity. Overseas demand for the products TTB regulates remains strong, with U.S. exports of all alcohol beverages totaling approximately $3.2 billion in 2012. The majority of these exports are spirits and wine products.

Promoting Fair Competition in the U.S. Marketplace

As part of its Trade Facilitation Program, TTB's FAA Act trade practices program investigates acts that violate federal law relating to alcohol beverage marketing practices. The FAA Act provisions that TTB enforces require TTB to ensure fair competition in the alcohol beverage trade by not only verifying

---

10 "*The Impact of Wine, Grapes and Grape Products on the American Economy 2007*," MKF Research LLC; "*The National Trade Association Representing Producers and Marketers of American's Favorite Brands of Distilled Spirits*," Distilled Spirits Council of the United States; "*Beer Industry Contributes Nearly $200 Billion to U.S. Economy*," Beer Institute and National Beer Wholesalers Association. Economic Impact study conducted by John Dunham & Associates, New York City, using data compiled in 2008.

that persons who engage in the trade are qualified to do so within the meaning of the statute, but also by ensuring that the trade practices among industry competitors comply with the law. Regulated trade practices include restrictions on exclusive outlets, tied house arrangements, commercial bribery, and consignment sales. Unlawful trade practices threaten fair competition by undermining equal access to the marketplace, precluding healthy small business activity, and limiting consumer choices by allowing influential producers to unlawfully interfere with the supply chain.

In FY 2013, TTB engaged in an evaluation of certain industry practices that may violate the tied house provisions of the FAA Act. These provisions provide that it is unlawful for an industry member to induce any retailer to purchase alcohol beverage products from the industry member to the exclusion, in whole or in part, of alcohol beverage products sold or offered for sale by other persons in interstate or foreign commerce. Examples of activities that are considered unlawful inducements under the FAA Act include furnishing, giving, renting, lending, or selling to the retailer any equipment, fixtures, signs, supplies, money, services, or other things of value. The regulatory exceptions to this provision are limited to certain promotional support items, such as product displays, point of sale advertising materials, equipment and supplies, and other items and services that are not considered to be an unlawful inducement.

In recent years, however, evolving industry practices and developing technologies have changed how shelf schematics are designed and offered to retailers. Shelf schematics in the current market are often complex computer-generated models of entire beverage sections that are increasingly offered in combination with shelf management programs that include additional related services, some of which could be considered unlawful inducements under the FAA Act. In FY 2013, TTB evaluated these programs and the use of shelf plans and schematics given by industry members to retailers in the current market to determine whether these practices constitute unlawful inducements. TTB intends to take additional actions to address this issue in FY 2014 to the extent that these activities violate federal laws that are intended to promote a competitive market by ensuring fair competition among industry members.

Facilitating U.S. Penetration into Foreign Markets

TTB has been actively engaged with U.S. trade officials in facilitating fair and open trade in alcohol beverages to support new opportunities for U.S. businesses in overseas markets. U.S. exports of alcohol beverages totaled more than $3 billion in 2012, the most recent full year of data available. In line with increases in overall export volume, alcohol beverage exports increased 17 percent compared to the prior calendar year. As the technical expert in these commodities, TTB seeks to promote U.S. exports by facilitating industry compliance with foreign requirements and by working with foreign regulators to address barriers that block market access for U.S. products.

TTB must process certificates for U.S. producers to facilitate export sales because many foreign countries require that shipments be accompanied by a certification from an appropriate government authority prior to allowing entry of the product. This activity affirms the integrity of domestically produced alcohol beverages and supports the U.S. trade policy goal to double exports by the end of 2014, as stated in the Administration's National Export Initiative.

For those countries that maintain a certification requirement, in FY 2013, TTB issued more than 10,000 export certificates for beer, wine, and distilled spirits. Without these certificates, which are only issued by TTB, U.S. producers of alcohol beverages cannot sell their products in major markets abroad. Through its international outreach and negotiations, TTB has arranged for the elimination or reduction of certification requirements for wine exported to the 27 member states of the European Union, Argentina, Australia, Canada, Chile, Georgia, New Zealand, and South Africa.

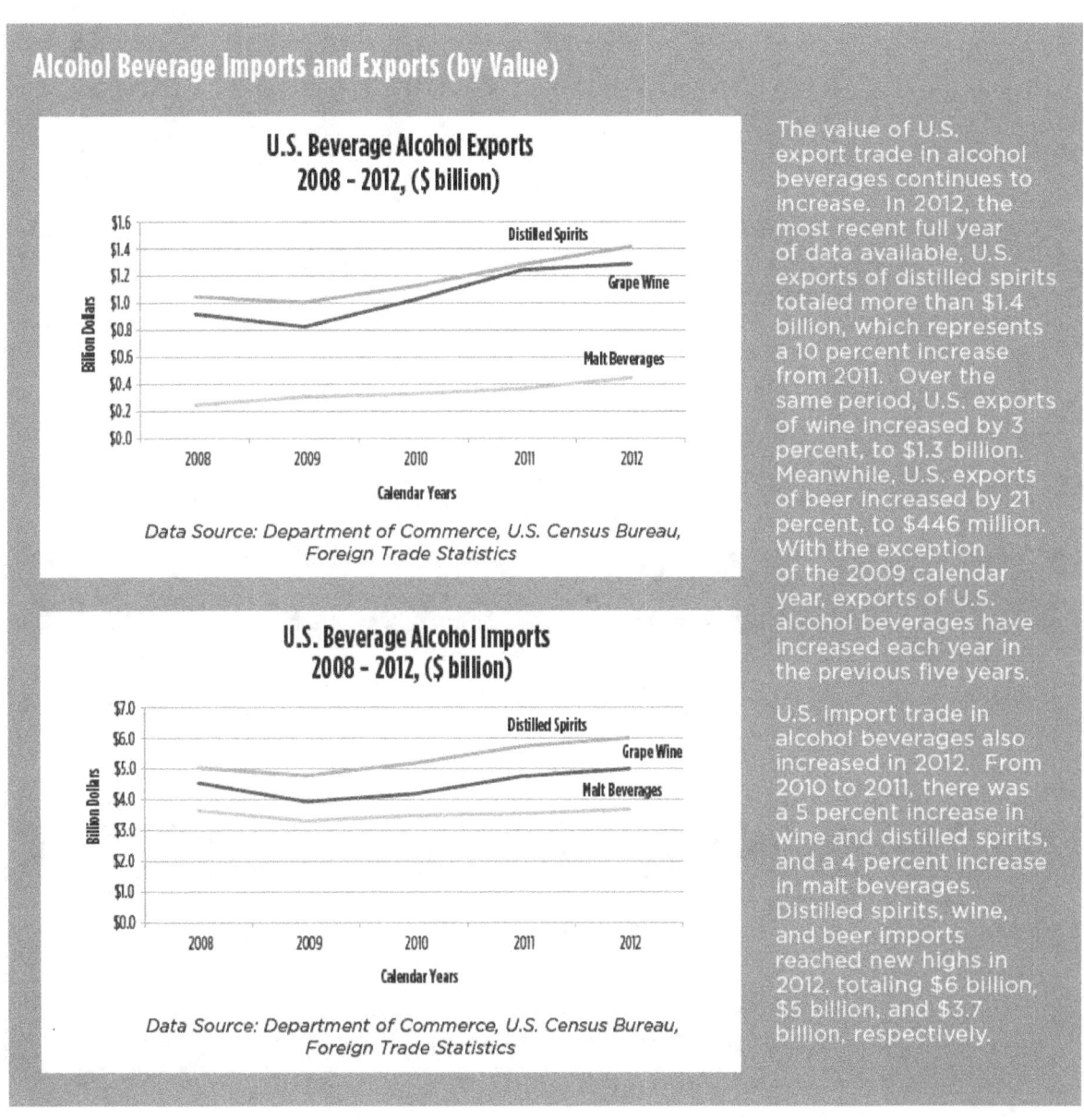

Alcohol Beverage Imports and Exports (by Value)

U.S. Beverage Alcohol Exports
2008 – 2012, ($ billion)

Data Source: Department of Commerce, U.S. Census Bureau, Foreign Trade Statistics

U.S. Beverage Alcohol Imports
2008 – 2012, ($ billion)

Data Source: Department of Commerce, U.S. Census Bureau, Foreign Trade Statistics

The value of U.S. export trade in alcohol beverages continues to increase. In 2012, the most recent full year of data available, U.S. exports of distilled spirits totaled more than $1.4 billion, which represents a 10 percent increase from 2011. Over the same period, U.S. exports of wine increased by 3 percent, to $1.3 billion. Meanwhile, U.S. exports of beer increased by 21 percent, to $446 million. With the exception of the 2009 calendar year, exports of U.S. alcohol beverages have increased each year in the previous five years.

U.S. import trade in alcohol beverages also increased in 2012. From 2010 to 2011, there was a 5 percent increase in wine and distilled spirits, and a 4 percent increase in malt beverages. Distilled spirits, wine, and beer imports reached new highs in 2012, totaling $6 billion, $5 billion, and $3.7 billion, respectively.

Alcohol Beverage Exports

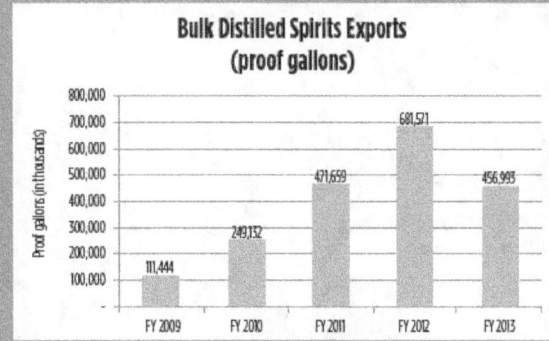

Bulk Distilled Spirits Exports (proof gallons)

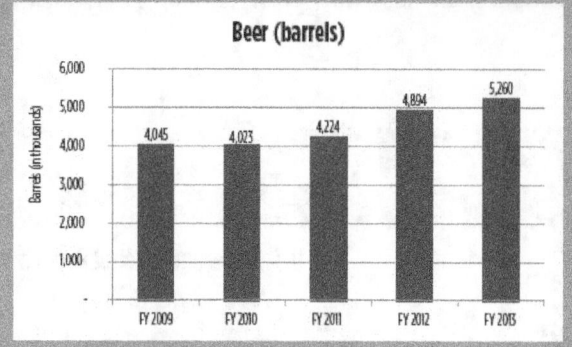

Beer (barrels)

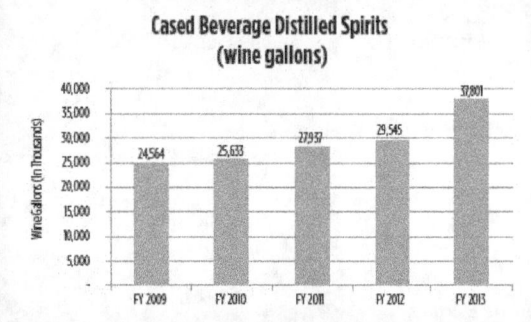

Cased Beverage Distilled Spirits (wine gallons)

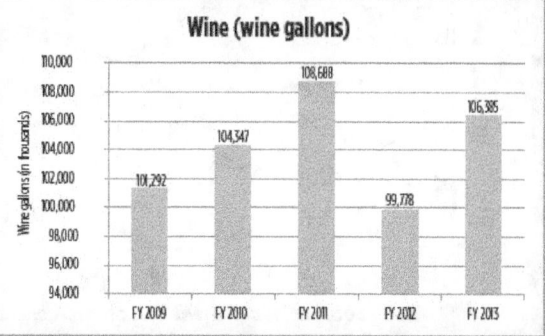

Wine (wine gallons)

Total Exports By Fiscal Year (in thousands)	FY 2009	FY 2010	FY 2011	FY 2012	FY 2013
Beverage Alcohol					
Beer (barrels)	4,045	4,023	4,224	4,894	5,260
Wine (wine gallons)	101,292	104,347	108,688	99,778	106,385
Bulk Distilled Spirits Exports (proof gallons)	111,444	249,132	471,659	681,571	456,993
Cased Beverage Distilled Spirits (wine gallons)	24,564	25,633	27,937	29,545	37,801

Percent Change from Prior Year	FY 2009	FY 2010	FY 2011	FY 2012	FY 2013
Beverage Alcohol					
Beer (barrels)	0.6%	−0.5%	5.0%	15.9%	7.5%
Wine (wine gallons)	−3.6%	3.0%	4.2%	−8.2%	6.6%
Bulk Distilled Spirits Exports (proof gallons)	−8.8%	123.5%	89.3%	44.5%	−33.0%
Cased Beverage Distilled Spirits (wine gallons)	−10.8%	4.4%	9.0%	5.8%	27.9%

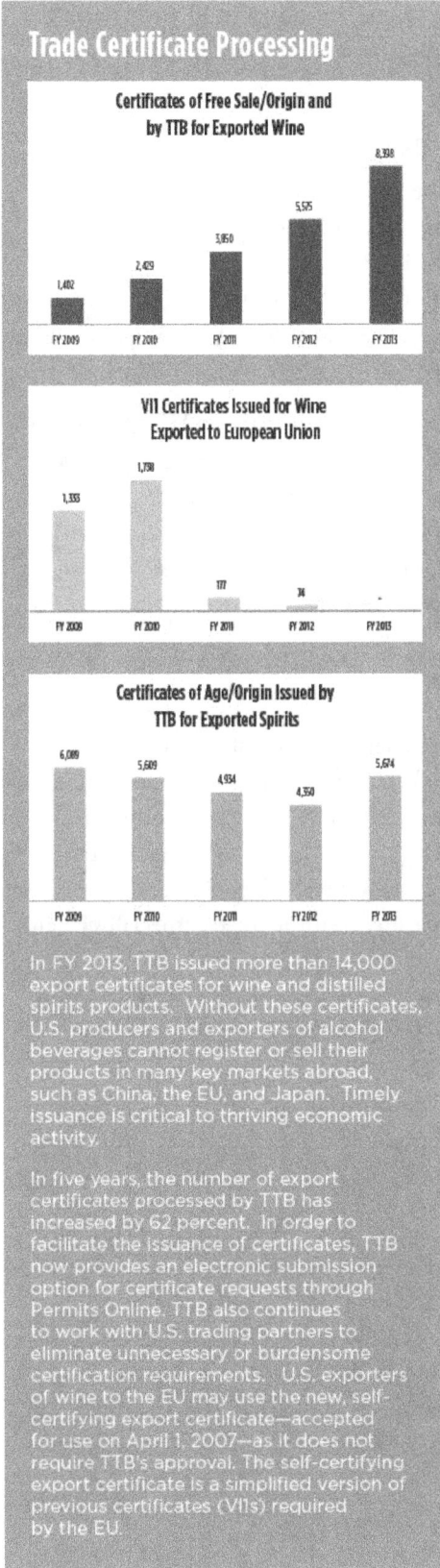

Trade Certificate Processing

Certificates of Free Sale/Origin and by TTB for Exported Wine

- FY 2009: 1,482
- FY 2010: 2,429
- FY 2011: 3,050
- FY 2012: 5,525
- FY 2013: 8,398

VI1 Certificates Issued for Wine Exported to European Union

- FY 2009: 1,333
- FY 2010: 1,791
- FY 2011: 177
- FY 2012: 74
- FY 2013: –

Certificates of Age/Origin Issued by TTB for Exported Spirits

- FY 2009: 6,089
- FY 2010: 5,609
- FY 2011: 4,934
- FY 2012: 4,350
- FY 2013: 5,674

In FY 2013, TTB issued more than 14,000 export certificates for wine and distilled spirits products. Without these certificates, U.S. producers and exporters of alcohol beverages cannot register or sell their products in many key markets abroad, such as China, the EU, and Japan. Timely issuance is critical to thriving economic activity.

In five years, the number of export certificates processed by TTB has increased by 62 percent. In order to facilitate the issuance of certificates, TTB now provides an electronic submission option for certificate requests through Permits Online. TTB also continues to work with U.S. trading partners to eliminate unnecessary or burdensome certification requirements. U.S. exporters of wine to the EU may use the new, self-certifying export certificate—accepted for use on April 1, 2007—as it does not require TTB's approval. The self-certifying export certificate is a simplified version of previous certificates (VI1s) required by the EU.

TTB's workload in processing export certificates increased by 62 percent between fiscal years 2009 and 2013, primarily reflecting the growth in U.S. wine and spirits exports. Exports of these alcohol beverage commodities increased approximately 50 percent between 2009 and 2012, from $2.1 billion to $3.2 billion, based on the most recent trade statistics.

China

The People's Republic of China is an important emerging market for U.S. alcohol beverage exporters and represents the single largest destination country for export certificates processed by TTB. In FY 2013, TTB issued more than 4,800 certificates for China-bound exports.

To streamline the operation and reduce paperwork for both sides of the U.S.-China wine trade, TTB proposed to China's Administration of Quality Supervision Inspection and Quarantine and the General Administration of Customs to use a one-page consolidated wine export certificate. In an 18-month period, TTB conducted multiple rounds of negotiations with AQSIQ to resolve several issues, including requirements for bottling dates, food additives, transportation information, and a description of the wine. In June 2013, TTB and Chinese officials reached an agreement on the content of the consolidated certificate. A start date for accepting the consolidated certificate at Chinese ports is to be determined.

Going forward, TTB will continue to seek agreements with additional U.S. trade partners to reduce or eliminate certification requirements where possible.

Preventing and Addressing Barriers to Trade

The TTB Trade Facilitation Program also includes identifying and addressing barriers to trade in the international marketplace. TTB is the principal advisor and technical expert for the Office of the United States Trade Representative (USTR) and other federal agencies in the administration of U.S. alcohol laws, regulations, and policies, and coordinates with these agencies as appropriate in responding to alcohol beverage and tobacco trade issues. TTB provides expert reviews of foreign regulatory proposals impacting the alcohol and tobacco trade to identify and assess the impact of potential trade barriers for U.S. alcohol and tobacco exporters. The USTR estimates that between 10 – 20 percent of new barriers to trade relate to alcohol beverages, and TTB plays a crucial role in the early identification and resolution of these issues.

World Trade Organization Committee Participation

Members of the World Trade Organization (WTO) are obligated to submit proposed, new, and amended technical regulations to the WTO for review and comment by other WTO members. The notification process prevents new non-tariff trade barriers. TTB participates in the interagency Technical Barriers to Trade (TBT) and Sanitary and Phytosanitary (SPS) Measures Working Group and provides its expertise on alcohol beverage regulations submitted to the WTO TBT Committee. In FY 2013, TTB addressed issues related to alcohol beverage regulations or standards proposed by the European Union, Israel, Russia, and Vietnam.

During FY 2013, TTB reviewed a total of 34 new regulatory measures submitted to the WTO SPS and TBT Committees related to alcohol beverages and, in conjunction with interagency partners, provided comments to the notifying country on 14 measures that presented potential technical trade barriers for U.S. producers. The measures TTB provided comments on included Colombian requirements on analytical parameters, oenological practices, and testing; Kenyan health warning statements; Mexican health warning statements; Nicaraguan technical regulations on rum; Peruvian requirements for adulterated beverages; and Vietnamese labeling requirements.

Codex Alimentarius Participation

TTB participates in Codex Alimentarius committee meetings to prevent this standards-setting organization from adopting new standards that would impede the U.S. export trade in alcohol beverages. The Codex Committee on Food Additives (CCFA) sets the maximum use levels of food additives through the General Standard on Food Additives (GSFA). Many developing countries look to the GSFA to set national legislation and do not allow additives that are not listed in the GSFA. This reliance on the GSFA has resulted in trade barriers for U.S. alcohol beverages entering certain markets, especially Japan and other Asian countries, because not all additives are currently on the GSFA list. In FY 2013, TTB served as the lead agency for the U.S. in a CCFA working group on wine additives. The working group is currently reviewing acidity regulators, emulsifiers, stabilizers, and thickeners for use in grape wine products, and CCFA will present its findings and recommendations in Hong Kong in March 2014. TTB will continue to work with CCFA to include other classes of food additives in the wine category of the GSFA as part of a multi-year project that will result in greatly reduced technical trade barriers for the U.S. wine industry.

Additionally, TTB participates in the Codex Committee on Food Labeling (CCFL). In FY 2013, the CCFL began working on issues related to date marking, which are of great concern to the U.S. alcohol industry based on the general position that wine and distilled spirits should not require date markings because these products usually do not spoil over time. TTB discussed the U.S. industry's concerns and received support from some countries to possibly exclude wine and distilled spirits from date marking requirements. Discussions on these issues will continue at the next meeting of the CCFL in Canada in November 2014. TTB will continue to seek an exemption from date marking labeling requirements for wines and distilled spirits.

Supporting International Trade Agreements for Alcohol Beverages

TTB also works to address barriers in the international marketplace by participating with other federal agencies in the negotiation of international trade agreements related to alcohol and tobacco products on behalf of the U.S. government.

Trans-Pacific Partnership Agreement

In FY 2013, TTB participated with the USTR in the negotiation of the Trans-Pacific Partnership Agreement (TPP). The TPP—a free-trade agreement being negotiated between Australia, Brunei, Canada, Chile, Japan, Malaysia, Mexico, New Zealand, Peru, Singapore, the United States, and Vietnam—includes a Wine and Spirits Annex in the chapter on technical barriers to trade. The Annex aims to reduce barriers to trade in the regulation of wine and spirits by laying out acceptable procedures in the areas of labeling, identity standards, conformity assessments, compliance periods, and acceptance of oenological practices. The President of the United States and other TPP leaders have called on negotiators to complete the agreement by the end of calendar year 2013.

European Union Agreements

The European Union (EU) is the top export market for U.S. wine, and it is the largest source of imported wine in the United States. As a result, maintaining a free flow of trade between the two economies is vital to U.S. economic growth.

In FY 2013, TTB participated in two bilateral meetings with representatives of the European Commission (EC) relating to the U.S.-EU Agreement on Trade in Wine. The meetings covered various trade issues, including the EU's:

- New standards for organic wine, which conflict with U.S. standards and resulted in U.S. exporters losing the ability to make certain organic claims on wine exported to the EU;

- Acceptance of electronic versions of the certificates that it requires for U.S. wine shipments to the EU;

- Restrictions on the use of certain "traditional terms" like "chateau," "clos," "ruby," and "tawny" on labels of U.S. wine exported to the EU; and

- Recent requirements that wine labels include allergen statements.

TTB also participated in two additional bilateral meetings relating to the U.S. - EU Organic Equivalency Agreement, during which the parties discussed issues concerning organic wine production and labeling.

Also in FY 2013, the EU and the U.S. announced the start of negotiations on the Transatlantic Trade and Investment Partnership (TTIP), which is a comprehensive free trade agreement between the two economies. TTB worked with the USTR to address alcohol beverage issues that may arise in negotiations on intellectual property, agricultural market access, and technical barriers to trade. TTB will continue to work with USTR on TTIP in FY 2014 to ensure protection of U.S. stakeholders' interests.

Asia-Pacific Economic Cooperation Wine Regulatory Forum

In FY 2013, TTB continued its work with interagency partners and U.S. industry to promote U.S. export trade in wine through the Asia-Pacific Economic Cooperation's (APEC) Wine Regulatory Forum. Through this project, TTB works with the USTR, the USDA Foreign Agricultural Service, the U.S.

Department of Commerce, and the U.S. Department of State to establish open dialogue and exchange of information with the APEC economies in support of expanding markets for U.S. exports. This forum is particularly important as emerging markets are creating increasing numbers of technical barriers to trade in alcohol beverages.

APEC is the premier forum for facilitating economic growth, cooperation, trade, and investment in the Asia-Pacific region.[11] The 21 APEC members are: Australia, Brunei Darussalam, Canada, Chile, the People's Republic of China, Hong Kong, Indonesia, Japan, the Republic of Korea, Malaysia, Mexico, New Zealand, Papua New Guinea, Peru, the Republic of the Philippines, Russia, Singapore, Chinese Taipei, the United States, Thailand, and Vietnam. Many of the APEC member economies are emerging export markets for the U.S. wine industry and this forum supports efforts to reduce the technical trade barriers to alcohol beverage trade created by these emerging markets.

In FY 2013, APEC announced its approval of a multi-year project proposal to address certain wine issues. The proposal, submitted to APEC by the United States and 11 co-sponsoring economies, would enhance the wine trade through the spread of good regulatory practices and improved regulatory capabilities across APEC. The proposal includes activities related to certification, technical workshops, information exchange, and collaboration on international standards. Moving forward, TTB will continue to work with APEC members to help those economies develop responsible regulatory activity that does not impede trade in alcohol beverages.

World Wine Trade Group

The U.S. is a participant in the World Wine Trade Group (WWTG), an informal grouping of government and industry representatives from the wine-producing countries of Argentina, Australia, Canada, Chile, Georgia, New Zealand, the United States, and South Africa. The WWTG, founded in 1998, aims to collaborate on a variety of international issues and create new opportunities for wine trade. Since its inception, the WWTG has completed a number of agreements related to oenological practices, labeling practices for wine, and trade certifications, all of which seek to minimize trade barriers and facilitate international trade.

In FY 2013, TTB accomplished several key objectives related to WWTG initiatives. In June 2013, TTB published a final rule that amended its regulations to permit the alcohol content statement to appear on other labels affixed to the container rather than requiring it to appear on the brand label. This rulemaking conforms the U.S. wine labeling regulations to the WWTG Agreement on Requirements for Wine Labeling, which was signed in 2007 by the United States and six other participants. The agreement aims to facilitate international wine trade by committing the parties to permit four pieces of common mandatory information—country of origin, product name, net contents, and alcohol content—to be presented in any single field of vision on a primary container of wine.

TTB also advised USTR during the drafting and negotiation of a Protocol to the 2007 labeling agreement, which addresses other labeling requirements such as alcohol tolerance, vintage, variety, and wine regions, with a view to concluding an additional wine labeling agreement to further streamline

---

11 APEC is an inter-governmental grouping that operates on the basis of non-binding commitments and open dialogue. Unlike the World Trade Organization or other multilateral trade bodies, APEC has no treaty obligations required of its participants. Decisions are reached by consensus and commitments are undertaken on a voluntary basis.

TTB Hosts Thai Delegation to Strengthen Global Tax Administration

In July 2013, TTB officials hosted a delegation from the Royal Thai Excise Department. The delegation met with officials from across the Bureau to learn more about how TTB administers U.S. excise tax laws and regulations relating to alcohol and tobacco. The International Tax and Investment Center, a non-profit organization that provides excise tax policy guidance to developing countries, organized the delegation's educational visit to the United States.

TTB officials shared information about TTB's approach to tax administration, the rulemaking process, current trends in excise tax fraud, and how the Bureau combats fraud. The delegation shared an overview of how they function and pointed out some trends and problems they face. The delegation also visited TTB's laboratory facilities to learn more about analyzing alcohol and tobacco products to determine correct tax classifications, and discussions were held regarding possible future scientific collaboration.

A delegation from the Royal Thai Excise Department met with TTB officials in Washington, D.C. in July 2013 to learn how TTB administers its alcohol and tobacco excise tax system.

the international wine trade. The WWTG participants concluded negotiations on the Protocol, with five member countries signing on.

TTB will continue to work with the USTR and its WWTG counterparts in FY 2014 to further the group's key objectives, including outreach to strategic markets and the minimization of technical trade barriers.

Coordinating with Foreign Counterparts to Extend Regulatory Controls

The global trade in alcohol beverages is active and increasing and, to be an effective regulator, TTB must seek innovative and efficient ways to achieve its consumer protection and revenue collection mission. One key strategy to ensure that U.S. businesses remain competitive on a global scale is through improved communication and information exchange with our trading partners. TTB's expansion of international agreements has fostered a global network of regulators in the alcohol and tobacco industries that ensure markets remain open and that illegal activity in the global trade is addressed promptly.

As part of an effort to protect consumers and to facilitate the import and export trade in alcohol beverages, TTB signed a memorandum of understanding with the Wine Australia Corporation (Wine Australia) in FY 2013. Wine Australia is an Australian government statutory authority that is responsible for export regulation and compliance, wine sector information and analysis, and negotiations with other countries to reduce trade barriers. As Australia is the third-largest source of imported wine in the United States after Italy and France, accounting for 14 percent of wine imports in 2010, Wine Australia is a key counterpart for TTB. Australia is also a partner of the United States in the WWTG, the APEC Wine Regulatory Forum, and in international technical collaboration on wine. As partners in those groups, TTB and Wine Australia work together to penetrate strategic foreign markets and to minimize technical barriers to international wine trade.

TTB and Wine Australia will build on these efforts in FY 2014, particularly with regard to a five-year project on good regulatory practices related to wine under the auspices of APEC.

Protecting U.S. Standards of Identity

In FY 2013, TTB published two final rules that recognized the standards of identity for distinctive products of other countries and, in turn, those countries recognized certain distinctive products of the U.S. in accordance with trade agreements with those countries. These agreements help to ensure the integrity of U.S. distilled spirits in foreign markets.

Cachaça

In February 2013, TTB published a final rule to recognize "Cachaça" as a type of rum and as a distinctive product of Brazil. This followed an agreement between representatives of Brazil and the U.S., signed on April 9, 2012, under which the U.S. would recognize Cachaça as a distinctive product of Brazil, and Brazil would recognize Bourbon Whiskey and Tennessee Whiskey as distinctive products of the U.S. The Brazilian government published a decree in its Official Register on March 27, 2013, recognizing Bourbon and Tennessee Whiskey as distinctive products of the U.S.

Pisco

In May 2013, TTB published a final rule to recognize Pisco as a type of brandy that must be manufactured in Peru or Chile in accordance with the laws and regulations of the country of manufacture. In doing so, TTB clarified the distinctive nature of this product and reinforced its commitment to the U.S.-Chile Free Trade and U.S.-Peru Trade Promotion Agreements, through which Chile and Peru recognized Bourbon Whiskey and Tennessee Whiskey as distinctive products of the U.S.

Pisco, a grape brandy, is the key ingredient in the Pisco sour, the national cocktail of both Peru and Chile.

Product Integrity

Consumer confidence is essential to ensuring that U.S. and world economies perform at their full economic potential. TTB is the federal agency responsible for carrying out provisions of the FAA Act that ensure that labeling and advertising of alcohol beverages provide adequate information to the consumer concerning the identity and quality of the product. This authority also calls for TTB to prevent misleading labeling or advertising that may result in consumer deception regarding the product.

This consumer protection function falls under TTB's Advertising, Labeling, and Product Safety Program. Before an alcohol beverage product can be sold in the United States, TTB reviews the product label to ensure that it contains all mandatory information and does not mislead the consumer. In addition, labels are reviewed for compliance with the Alcohol Beverage Labeling Act, the federal law that mandates that a health warning statement appear on all alcohol beverages offered for sale and distribution in the United

Improving Product Information for Consumers

In FY 2013, TTB published Ruling 2013-2, Voluntary Nutrient Content Statements in the Labeling and Advertising of Wines, Distilled Spirits, and Malt Beverages, which allowed the use of voluntary nutrient content statements, or "Serving Facts" statements, in the labeling and advertising of wines, distilled spirits, and malt beverages. Industry members may now voluntarily provide truthful, accurate, specific, and non-misleading information to consumers about the serving size, the number of servings per container, the number of calories, and the number of grams of carbohydrates, protein, and fat per serving size. Voluntary Serving Facts statements may also include the alcohol content of a product as a percentage of alcohol by volume as well as by the number of fluid ounces of alcohol per serving. Industry members do not need to apply to TTB for a new COLA to add a Serving Facts statement to an existing label if the statement is consistent with one of the examples provided in TTB's guidance.

Serving Facts

Serving Size	5 fl oz (148 ml)
Servings Per Container	5

Amount Per Serving	
Alcohol by volume	14%
fl oz of alcohol	0.7
Calories	120
Carbohydrate	3g
Fat	0g
Protein	0g

An example of an acceptable Serving Facts statement for a 750 milliliter bottle of wine containing 14 percent alcohol by volume. This example includes the optional percent by volume alcohol content declaration as well as the optional declaration of alcohol in fluid ounces.

States. The approved label application is called a Certificate of Label Approval (COLA).

TTB confirms compliance with federal product and labeling regulations by reviewing production records through its product integrity investigations and by conducting marketplace sampling to test products for safety as well as container content and label compliance. TTB also reviews advertisements for alcohol beverage products from television, radio, the Internet, and other sources for compliance with federal regulations.

In the event that a food safety or other product integrity issue occurs, TTB responds by working directly with the responsible parties and, as appropriate, shares its findings with other regulatory and enforcement agencies and works in partnership to timely resolve the issue.

Modernizing the Alcohol Beverage Label Program

TTB continues to modernize its alcohol beverage labeling program through three main initiatives: 1) improving the label application submission process, 2) providing clear guidance to industry, and 3) random sampling of alcohol beverage products in the marketplace to enhance enforcement efforts and track compliance. These initiatives will facilitate TTB's planned shift in focus from pre-market approvals of alcohol beverage labels to a more useful marketplace review of labels.

Label Application Submissions

TTB continues to implement improvements to the label application process to help support timely processing and ensure that TTB does not interfere with compliant trade. Annual increases in label applications and resource challenges have made prompt service difficult to maintain. The number of applications for label approval that TTB received between fiscal years 2008 and 2012 increased 14 percent. After a decline in FY 2009, the number of label filings trended up again in fiscal years 2010 through 2012, sparked by industry growth and product innovation. Processing times have been delayed as a result, with the average time for a label approval reaching 31 days in FY 2013, up 35 percent compared to the average of 23 days in FY 2012.

Over the same period, industry members increasingly relied on COLAs Online to electronically file their label applications. Nearly 92 percent of all COLA applications in FY 2013 were submitted to TTB via COLAs Online. TTB has continued to introduce system enhancements to draw industry members to electronic filing, including updating processing information and adding new system validations to check the completeness of applications. Technology enhancements alone will not entirely address the strain on TTB resources presented by the high volume of label applications and scarce resources to process them.

In FY 2013, however, the label application curve shifted downwards, with an 8 percent decrease in label applications submitted to TTB, dropping from 152,741 in FY 2012 to 140,324 in FY 2013. TTB attributes this reduction in label applications to its steps to increase the number of changes that manufacturers and importers may make to their alcohol beverage label without seeking a new label approval. The expanded list includes 28 permissible revisions, which include repositioning label information. These changes continue to place a check on the rising number of label applications, and TTB will continue to examine options to reduce the burden on industry while maintaining its public protection responsibilities.

TTB also issued guidance to the beer industry in TTB Ruling 2013-1 to clarify that malt beverages sold exclusively in intrastate commerce do not require a COLA unless the state requires brewers to do so. Because many brewers produce, bottle, and sell their products within the same state, TTB anticipates that this clarification will reduce the number of label applications submitted by many brewers.

Federal Labeling Regulations

In FY 2013, in line with providing industry with clear guidance, TTB continued its efforts to modernize the federal alcohol beverage labeling regulations. By modernizing the labeling regulations to remove ambiguity and to remain current with market conditions, TTB anticipates that industry will gain greater understanding of federal requirements, resulting in increased label compliance. These efforts should help industry avoid the administrative burden and cost of multiple application resubmissions, and promote the most efficient use of TTB's resources. TTB will continue to develop the notice of proposed rulemaking for revisions to the federal labeling regulations for beer, wine, and distilled spirits products to reflect the current alcohol beverage market and industry practices through FY 2014, with an anticipated publication date in early FY 2015.

Market Review of Label and Product Compliance

After alcohol beverages enter the marketplace, TTB monitors labeling compliance through the Alcohol Beverage Sampling Program (ABSP). The ABSP is a random survey of products in the marketplace to help TTB evaluate marketplace compliance and determine where compliance issues exist. The Bureau's continued monitoring of product and label compliance through the ABSP assists TTB in evaluating the integrity of U.S. alcohol beverage products, both in the view of U.S. consumers and TTB's international counterparts, which is critical to gaining foreign market access for U.S. exporters.

For the random sample of products included in ABSP, TTB determines if they are fully and accurately labeled (i.e., whether the label accurately reflects the content of the bottle) by reviewing the labels and contents of those products. In reviewing the label, TTB checks for all required information and determines if there is a valid COLA. TTB also sends the products to its laboratories to undergo chemical analyses to evaluate whether the label information accurately reflects the content of the container.

TTB uses the ABSP results to address compliance problems for products that are currently in the marketplace. In most cases, TTB notifies the industry member about a violation and works with them to bring the product into compliance. For more significant violations, however, the Bureau conducts field investigations and follows up with industry members. Significant violations that required TTB field intervention in FY 2013 included wines that were misclassified for tax purposes and a case involving possible COLA fraud. The complete results of the FY 2013 ABSP will be available on TTB.gov in early FY 2014.

ABSP results over the past few years indicate that accurate proofing and gauging for distilled spirits is an issue for a significant number of industry members. Because the excise tax for distilled spirits is based on alcohol content, proper gauging of distilled spirits is integral to proper tax determination. To address this issue, TTB is developing online educational tools in FY 2014 to assist distillers with their gauging skills.

Modernizing the Formula Application Process

TTB reviews domestic and imported alcohol beverage formulations to support accurate labeling of alcohol beverages, as well as appropriate tax classification. Formulas include statements of process, laboratory analyses, and pre-import letters, all of which function to ensure U.S. consumers have full and accurate information about the products they purchase.

Formula applications have increased rapidly in recent years for all alcohol beverage commodities, with the volume of submissions doubling in the past five years. Formula applications increased another 7 percent between FY 2012 to FY 2013. This increase is due to the overall growth in the alcohol beverage market as well as trends toward more flavored distilled spirits, wines, and malt beverages. In addition, craft brewers and craft distillers are increasingly creating new and innovative products or using non-traditional methods to distinguish their products. Industry members are required to submit the formulas for these products to TTB for review to verify that the products are appropriately labeled and do not pose a risk to consumer safety.

TTB is addressing this dramatic increase in the number of formula applications by modernizing the formulation program through improved regulatory guidance and an enhanced online submission process. In FY 2013, TTB issued guidance for the beer industry to clarify that certain ingredients and processes are exempt from formula requirements under the beer regulations. Given that the number of brewers in the U.S. increased by more than 35 percent in FY 2013, TTB anticipates that this guidance will help reduce the burden for brewers associated with the formula application and approval process and stem the increase of formula applications submitted to TTB. In FY 2014, TTB will continue to evaluate whether additional ingredients or processes for beer may be exempted from the formula approval requirement, and TTB intends to pursue the modernization of the formula requirements for beer, wine, and distilled spirits through regulatory action within the next several years.

TTB also made progress in modernizing the formula application process in FY 2013 through implementing multiple improvements to Formulas Online, the online system that allows industry members to submit and track formula applications electronically. Formulas Online also allows industry members to link their approved alcohol beverage formulas to COLAs Online when they file for COLAs. In FY 2013, TTB received 73 percent of its formula applications electronically, an increase of 24 percent in just one year. Continued system enhancements and outreach are driving higher adoption rates. The FY 2013 improvements to Formulas Online included several key features to improve the user experiences, included improvements to user registration, enhanced search functionality, and improved user notifications.

TTB is engaging industry to ensure its next phase of system enhancements is responsive to user feedback. In FY 2013, TTB hosted three Formulas Online Improvement Forums with industry representatives to discuss recent enhancements to Formulas Online and to share and gather ideas for future improvements. These forums provided a valuable opportunity for dialogue between industry and TTB and assist TTB in prioritizing future enhancements. In FY 2014, TTB will continue to conduct forums and enhance Formulas Online to provide an even more efficient and user-friendly electronic filing venue for both industry and TTB.

Protecting Consumers from Adulterated and Contaminated Products

In administering the Advertising, Labeling, and Product Safety Program, TTB also conducts routine analyses of sampled alcohol beverages for ingredients or materials whose presence is prohibited or limited. Examples include thujone and toxic heavy metals. Additional examples include wines that are analyzed to ensure safe levels of pesticides and ochratoxin-A, and malt beverages that are tested for mycotoxins, among other things. TTB also works with its counterpart U.S. agencies to evaluate and address incidents involving potential health hazards related to alcohol beverage products, including the Food and Drug Administration (FDA). TTB considers an adulterated alcohol beverage product, as defined by the Federal Food, Drug, and Cosmetic Act and determined by the FDA, to be mislabeled under Federal alcohol beverage labeling laws.

In FY 2013, TTB became aware of high levels of phthalates in a Chinese baijiu product, which is a distilled spirit made from sorghum and other grains. Phthalates are synthetic chemicals with a broad spectrum of uses, including as an additive to plastic to increase flexibility and durability. Certain phthalates have been linked to adverse developmental and reproductive effects, which has raised concerns among the public and regulators due to their widespread use. To assess whether the phthalate issue was isolated to the identified product, TTB obtained samples of baijiu products for analysis by TTB's Beverage Alcohol Laboratory. TTB found phthalates in the identified product at higher levels than the other baijiu products. TTB is currently working with the importer to determine the source of the phthalates and coordinating with FDA and its phthalates task force to conduct a health hazard evaluation for phthalates in distilled spirits products.

Also in FY 2013, TTB worked with industry members on the voluntary recall of several alcohol beverage products, including a gin product that was found to contain glass particles and a distilled spirits specialty product made from vodka and sparkling wine that did not have the required sulfite allergen disclosure on its label. In each instance, TTB worked with other agencies and the affected industry members to monitor and confirm resolution of the voluntary recalls, and no adverse health impacts to the public were reported.

Voluntary Compliance

In its Collect the Revenue and Protect the Public programs, TTB promotes voluntary compliance by providing clearer regulatory standards and guidance, encouraging use of its e-Gov filing systems, and supporting industry members through education and outreach efforts. TTB employees provide industry members and states with direct assistance on specific needs or guidance on broader issues affecting the regulated commodities.

Supporting Compliance through Industry Outreach

The industries regulated by TTB are growing rapidly, and obtaining voluntary compliance requires that TTB educate both new and existing industry members on federal requirements in the areas of manufacturing, marketing, importing, and exporting alcohol and tobacco products, as well as on paying tax on alcohol, tobacco, firearms, and ammunition products. TTB has reshaped its approach to outreach in recent years to operate a voluntary compliance program with limited resources by taking advantage of technological advances. Although TTB continues to attend select industry-sponsored seminars and workshops to provide information and answer questions on federal laws and regulations, TTB increasingly relies on online training to reach industry members. These online training materials are published for industry to reference in the future.

TTB employees participated in the Unified Wine and Grape Symposium in Sacramento, California in January 2013. The symposium is one of the largest of its kind, with more than 13,000 attendees. TTB operated an information booth and presented on topics ranging from how to enter the wine industry, to compliance, labeling, and international issues.

In FY 2013, TTB held several Webinars for industry members that were intended to promote awareness of recent updates to the alcohol beverage label approval process and to support increased adoption rates for TTB's e-Gov filing solutions. To help inform industry members and state regulators about the expansion of the allowable revisions list, TTB provided detailed formal guidance regarding the allowable revisions on TTB.gov and conducted five webinars in FY 2013. These webinars promoted the expansion of the allowable revisions list and explained how reducing the number of COLA applications that TTB receives relates to COLA application processing times. TTB also delivered three Webinars in 2013 to promote use of Formulas Online for the submission of nonbeverage formula applications. TTB targeted these Webinars to the approximately 35 percent of nonbeverage alcohol producers who had never used Formulas Online, with content directed specifically to flavor manufacturers, specially denatured alcohol users, and dietary supplement manufacturers.

In FY 2013, TTB also continued to raise awareness of the Pay.gov system for filing tax returns and operational reports, an important strategy to improve compliance rates as the system facilitates the submission of complete and accurate filings. A multi-faceted effort was implemented across TTB to promote Pay.gov use, which included outreach at industry events and seminars, system enhancements, and targeted education efforts for industry members not yet registered in the system. In FY 2013, TTB also increased the number of TTB tax-related forms available via Pay.gov and streamlined the automatic registration of new industry members. These outreach efforts and system enhancements contributed to increased rates of industry members using the system to electronically submit operational reports and tax returns in FY 2013. At year-end, 23 percent of excise tax returns and 35 percent of operational reports were submitted through Pay.gov, an increase of 1 – 2 percent in the electronic filing of returns and reports. To increase use of Pay.gov in the future, in FY 2013, TTB began discussions with the Bureau of the Fiscal Service, which operates Pay.gov, about enabling the system to accept credit card payments from TTB taxpayers. This enhancement would also address a timing issue that currently requires those who file electronically to remit tax payments early.

Improving Access to Online Guidance

TTB has long relied on TTB.gov as a primary means of sharing information and announcements with its industry members. In FY 2013, the Bureau developed and launched a TTB.gov mobile application—TTB Mobile—to improve customer access to critical information from hand-held mobile devices. The expectations of the business community TTB serves are changing in response to the revolution in mobile technology. Today, approximately 12 percent of TTB.gov visitors are using a mobile device to access the TTB Web site, an increase of 9 percent over the prior year and growing.

TTB designed its mobile site to make navigation on smartphones and other hand-held mobile devices faster and more user-friendly, as informed by the demographics, habits, and trends of those who visit TTB.gov most often. For industry members, the mobile site provides access to TTB.gov's most common tasks, such as general inquiries on applying for a permit, getting label approval, import and export requirements, and paying taxes. It also provides instant access to popular topics and public guidance. For TTB's increasingly mobile workforce, TTB Mobile provides convenient access to all of the Bureau's regulatory information, guidance, and forms.

The TTB Mobile application improves access to key information on TTB.gov.

TTB Mobile is supported by a wide variety of platforms and devices, including iPhone, Android, Blackberry, and Windows Mobile. This initiative also supports Treasury's broader aims in its Digital Government Strategy to optimize public-facing services.

Issuing Guidance on Social Media Advertising

TTB's authorities to prevent consumer deception extend to the advertising of alcohol beverages. The federal regulations for each commodity outline the mandatory information that must appear in advertising and list the statements and practices that are prohibited from appearing in advertising materials.

In enforcing compliance, TTB routinely reviews advertisements that appear in various media, including print, television, outdoor, and Web site advertisements. Advances in technology have led to the development of new forms of advertising (i.e., social media) that are interactive, allowing consumers and industry members to generate content and create links between various social media outlets. These outlets include social network services such as Facebook, video sharing sites such as YouTube, blogs, online forums or comment sections, and applications for mobile devices. With the emergence and growth of these types of media outlets, TTB is expanding the breadth of its advertising reviews.

TTB has found over the past few years that more industry members are using social media to advertise their products, and often these advertisements are missing mandatory information or contain information that is prohibited. In response, TTB issued Industry Circular 2013–1, Use of Social Media in the Advertising of Alcohol Beverages, to assist industry members in ensuring that their advertisements appearing in social media outlets comply with federal advertising regulations. The circular advises industry members that all advertisements of wine, distilled spirits, and malt beverages in any media, including social media, must comply with federal requirements regarding both mandatory statements and prohibited practices or statements.

Streamlining Regulations to Reduce the Compliance Burden

TTB seeks to promote voluntary compliance by ensuring that the regulated industry has all the tools needed to incorporate compliance as part of their business models, including clear and unambiguous regulations and guidance. TTB has an ongoing regulations modernization effort underway to ensure that its regulations and enforcement strategy keep up with changes in the industries that it regulates. In FY 2013, TTB made significant progress in updating its regulations to reflect current industry practices and achieve efficiencies for the industry and TTB.

TTB is currently engaged in rulemaking to consolidate the required distilled spirits plant (DSP) monthly operations reports. In its original proposal, published in FY 2012, TTB proposed replacing the current four report forms that DSPs use to report their operations with two new forms that they would submit monthly, or quarterly if they qualify to file taxes on a quarterly basis. Based on public comments, TTB currently is preparing to issue a supplemental proposed rulemaking that will propose to replace the current four operations report forms with just one form, which would be filed on a monthly or quarterly basis as described above. TTB undertook this project to address numerous concerns and desires for improved reporting by the affected distilled spirits industry members and to achieve efficiencies by reducing the number of monthly plant operations reports that DSPs must complete and file, and that TTB must process. TTB intends to continue this rulemaking project in FY 2014.

In FY 2013, TTB also continued a rulemaking project to revise the specially denatured alcohol (SDA) and completely denatured alcohol (CDA) formula regulations. SDA and CDA are widely used in the U.S. fuel, medical, and manufacturing sectors. The industrial alcohol industry is far larger than the beverage alcohol industry in both size and scope, and it continues to grow in the U.S. Based upon a determination that certain products present minimal revenue risk, TTB issued a proposed rulemaking in June 2013 that proposes to eliminate outdated SDA formulas from the regulations, reclassify some SDA formulas as CDA, and issue new general-use formulas for products made with SDA to reduce the number of products that require pre-approval by TTB. TTB estimates that this effort will decrease the number of formula submissions required from industry by an estimated 80 percent. These changes would remove

Specially denatured and completely denatured alcohol are distilled spirits to which materials have been added to render the spirits unfit for beverage use.

TTB Laboratories Renew International Accreditation

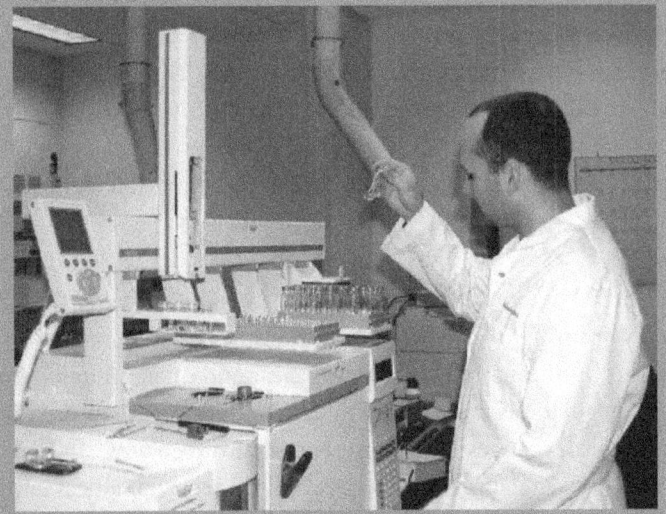

In FY 2013, the National Laboratory Center in Beltsville, Maryland and the Compliance Laboratory in Walnut Creek, California, renewed their International Organization for Standardization (ISO) 17025 accreditation from the American Association for Laboratory Accreditation.

Through accreditation, TTB's laboratories achieve third-party recognition of their quality results. Accreditation reduces inefficiencies and puts mechanisms in place for continuous improvement.

The ISO is a non-governmental organization that promotes the development of standardization to facilitate the international exchange of goods and services. ISO accreditation promotes recognition and respect for TTB laboratories' technical competence from industry and other agencies, both nationally and internationally.

The ISO 17025 standard specifically applies to testing and calibration laboratories, and includes management and technical requirements.
To maintain accreditation, TTB's laboratories are audited every two years. Both laboratory locations have maintained accreditation since 2007.

unnecessary regulatory burdens and update the regulations to align them with current industry practice. TTB expects to publish a final rule in FY 2014.

Finally, in FY 2013, TTB pursued regulatory changes to encourage more small brewers to file their tax returns, tax payments, and operations reports on a quarterly basis, thereby reducing the filings required of industry and received by TTB annually. As the bond amount is considered to be the limiting factor in increasing quarterly filings, TTB published a temporary rule in December 2012 that reduced to $1,000 the penal sum for a brewer's bond for certain small brewers. With the temporary rule, TTB concurrently published a notice of proposed rulemaking (NPRM) that proposed to permanently reduce the amount of the bond required for small brewers to a flat rate of $1,000 and to require those brewers to quarterly file their tax returns, tax payments, and reports of operations. This effort is expected to facilitate quarterly filing by approximately 91 percent of all brewers and, according to a comment on the proposed rulemaking from the Brewers Association, to save small and independent American brewers $2 million annually. TTB plans to publish a final rule in FY 2014.

Moving forward, TTB will continue to modernize its regulations to make positive changes to the regulatory framework, which TTB believes will improve voluntary compliance by industry and significantly enhance TTB's accomplishment of its mission.

Performance Summary

Collect the Revenue

TTB met all of its performance measures under the ***Collect the Revenue*** activity. A detailed summary of TTB performance is discussed in Part II of this report, Program Performance Results.

Investments in the Collect the Revenue mission resulted in the following accomplishments in FY 2013:

Tax Collection

- TTB collected $22.9 billion in excise taxes and other revenues from approximately 9,300[12] taxpayers in the alcohol, tobacco, firearms, and ammunition industries. In all, TTB returned $457 for every $1 expended on tax collection activities.[13] Since the tax rate increase on tobacco products took effect, the return on TTB tax collection activities has increased by approximately 46 percent.

- TTB continued to expand its e-filing capability to enable all excise taxpayers to file and pay taxes, and file monthly operational reports, electronically through the Pay.gov system. In FY 2013, TTB streamlined the Pay.gov registration process for newly permitted industry members, increasing the total number of registered system users by 15 percent to more than 10,900. As registered Pay.gov users increase, TTB has targeted its outreach efforts to promote its use by these taxpayers. TTB made modest progress in FY 2013, increasing e-filed tax returns to 23 percent and e-filed operational reports to 35 percent.

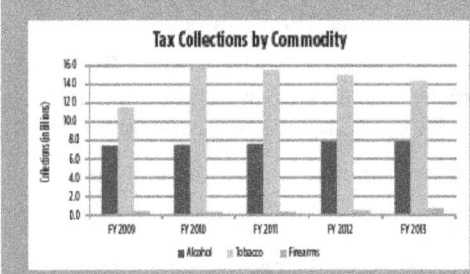

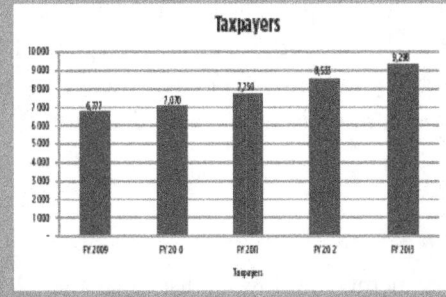

Total TTB tax collections trended down for the third consecutive year due to declining tobacco revenue. Tobacco tax collections reached an all-time high in FY 2010, the first full year of collections under the new federal tobacco tax rates, and have steadily decreased due to price conscious consumers switching from high tax products to low tax products, reduced tobacco consumption, and tax evasion challenges. Even with this decline, since 2008, tobacco revenues collected by TTB have increased 109 percent.

Alcohol tax revenue remained relatively constant compared to FY 2012, while FAET revenues continue to rise, with total collections up 49 percent compared to the prior year.

TTB regulates approximately 66,600 permittees, but only a small percentage file a return and pay taxes in a given fiscal year. The largest segment of TTB permit holders— alcohol importers and wholesalers—do not pay taxes to TTB. Following several years of modest growth, the TTB tax base grew nearly 10 percent for the third consecutive fiscal year. Since 2009, the number of TTB-regulated taxpayers has increased 37 percent.

---

12 Of the 15,475 TTB permittees whose business operations are subject to federal excise taxes, approximately 9,300 (60 percent) had activity that required them to file a tax return and pay excise tax in FY 2013.

13 TTB calculates its return on investment for its tax collection function by comparing total annual tax revenue to the annual appropriations obligated for tax collection activities.

Tax Classification

- The tax code does not provide clear standards to differentiate certain tobacco products, creating the potential for misclassification and erroneous tax payment on these products. The increased federal tax rates on cigarettes and other tobacco products has highlighted the importance of TTB's work to ensure the appropriate tax classification of tobacco products. The TTB Tobacco Laboratory analyzes tobacco samples in support of tobacco tax classification, tax fraud investigations, and in the development of protocols for counterfeit tobacco product authentication. The laboratory's work also supports regulatory projects to improve tobacco regulation and support effective tax enforcement. In FY 2013, TTB's laboratory advanced tobacco science by contributing to international studies on humectant concentration levels in tobacco products by the World Health Organization and its Tobacco Laboratory Network, a global network of the tobacco enforcement laboratories of more than 100 countries. Humectants, such as glycerol, propylene glycol, and triethylene glycol, are often added to tobacco products to retain moisture and increase shelf life. Humectant concentration is one of the objective criteria proposed by TTB to support potential rulemaking to better define tax classification standards for roll-your-own (RYO) and pipe tobacco. Participating and completing the validation study provides an internationally recognized consensus method for analysis of humectants in tobacco products.

- The tax differential on certain tobacco products contributed to the proliferation of cigarette manufacturing machines for consumer use. Legislation enacted in July 2012 (H.R. 4348) addressed the legal status of retailers that provide so-called RYO machines to customers. The law clarified that such manufacturers are required to apply for a permit from TTB, as well as pay federal excise taxes and comply with other federal regulatory requirements. TTB issued public guidance in October 2012 to clarify the applicable statutory and regulatory requirements for those operating RYO machines. The guidance also clarified that non-profit organizations, social clubs, cooperatives, and other similar organizations that made RYO machines available to members were not exempt from these requirements. In early FY 2013, TTB initiated enforcement action through letter notices to approximately 1,300 locations suspected of illegally operating RYO cigarette machines. In FY 2013, this TTB enforcement initiative resulted in the identification of approximately $1 million in tax liabilities and the initiation of several criminal investigations.

- TTB also analyzes nonbeverage and beverage alcohol samples to assign or verify a tax classification. For this purpose, in FY 2013, TTB chemists processed approximately 1,600 specially denatured alcohol formulas and samples to support tax-free alcohol claims. TTB analyzed another 1,200 beverage alcohol samples associated with pre-import evaluation, the 5010 tax credit, and enforcement activities. Pre-import evaluations also serve to protect consumers, as the analytical tests also analyze products for limited or prohibited ingredients.

Civil Tax Enforcement

- During FY 2013, TTB identified high-risk activity and industry members using sophisticated analytical techniques and completed approximately 520 audits, examinations, and revenue investigations. These enforcement efforts resulted in a total of $38.8 million in identified tax liabilities, with $17.6 million collected to date.

- Due to the known revenue risk in the import and export trade in alcohol and tobacco products, and as the federal permitting authority for alcohol and tobacco importers, TTB initiated an importer enforcement initiative driven by newly developed and deployed risk models. Between fiscal years 2012 and 2013, TTB conducted investigations of alcohol and tobacco importers that resulted in the identification of approximately $1.6 million in evaded federal excise taxes.

- TTB leverages its enforcement resources through partnerships with other regulatory and enforcement agencies. During FY 2013, TTB and CBP's Office of Regulatory Audit conducted a joint audit of a tobacco importer. This pilot case resulted in findings that the importer had failed to pay $6.3 million in federal excises due, and TTB is working with CBP on collecting the revenue due on the imported tobacco products. This effort also resulted in the development and implementation of new protocols between TTB and CBP for tax collections on TTB-regulated commodities. To date, CBP has initiated several tax collection actions under the new referral procedures, with $2.4 million at issue in those cases.

- In FY 2013, TTB continued its multi-year enforcement initiative related to manufacturers and importers of processed tobacco, as these are newly permitted entities that trade in a non-taxpaid tobacco product. In 2009, lawmakers enacted legislation to require that tobacco processors obtain a TTB permit and report on the first removal, transfer, or sale of processed tobacco to another entity. The transfer of this non-taxpaid tobacco product carries a high risk to federal revenue, as there are no restrictions on the sale of processed tobacco and only limited reporting requirements. To identify tax loss and potential criminal activity, TTB investigations trace processed tobacco from the point of removal by the permittee through the distribution chain, and have found that the product is being used in illicit manufacturing of tobacco products. Since beginning this enforcement initiative, TTB's audits and investigations have identified approximately $180 million in potential tax liabilities.

- TTB's processed tobacco forward trace investigations also identified a growing underground market for whole leaf tobacco used to manufacture "blunt" wrappers to smoke marijuana. The whole leaf tobacco, known as Grabba or Fronto Leaf, is sold to the consumer, who then removes the stem and cuts the leaf into squares used to roll marijuana cigarettes or "blunts." The whole leaf tobacco itself is not subject to federal regulation; however, the resulting blunt wrappers are regulated by TTB and the act of manufacturing the wrapper would require a permit and tax payment.

Criminal Tax Enforcement

- TTB has criminal enforcement authority over the commodities it taxes and regulates. Tax fraud in these industries, whether through unlawful product diversion or other means, poses a high risk to federal revenues. Diversion includes tax evasion, theft, distribution of counterfeit products, and distribution in the United States of products marked for export or for use outside the U.S. Since October 2010, TTB has reimbursed the IRS Criminal Investigation office for special agents to operate a law enforcement program to counteract illicit trade in the alcohol and tobacco industries. In just three years of operations, TTB agents have opened 64 cases for investigation, 17 of which were opened in FY 2013. The total estimated tax liability associated with these cases is nearly $350 million, with an additional $117 million in seizures and forfeitures. TTB had a higher than 94 percent acceptance rate for cases presented to an Assistant U.S. Attorney in FY 2013, with a 100 percent conviction rate in all completed cases. The total amount of tax loss at issue in cases recommended for prosecution in FY 2013 exceeded $57 million.

FY 2013 Tax Collections by State

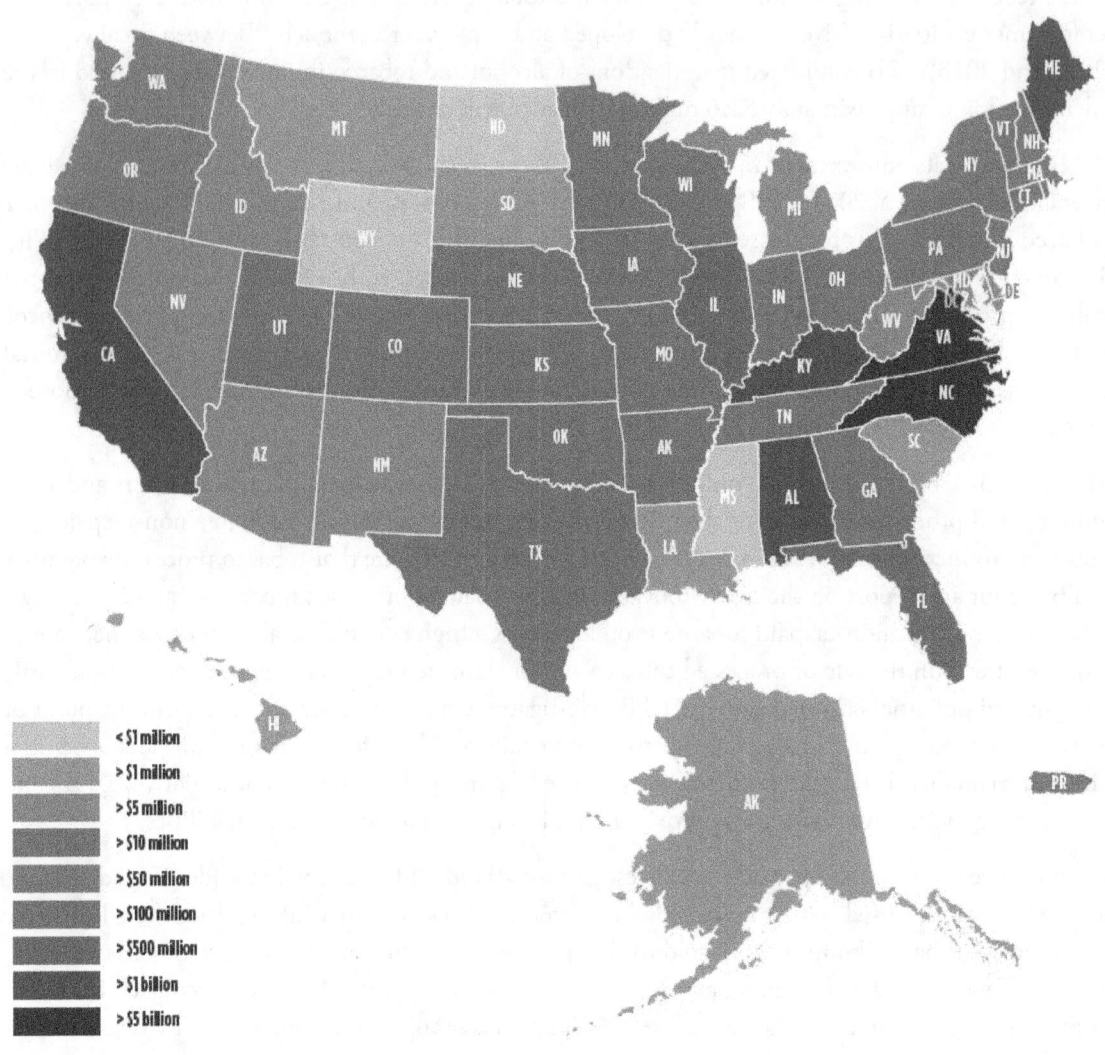

Legend:
- < $1 million
- > $1 million
- > $5 million
- > $10 million
- > $50 million
- > $100 million
- > $500 million
- > $1 billion
- > $5 billion

States* with the Largest Percentage Increase in Federal Excise Tax Collections

State	FY 2009	FY 2013	% Increase
AL	$11,812,582	$60,342,919	411%
NV	$3,020,147	$7,831,778	159%
MI	$3,372,597	$8,505,428	145%
NE	$6,746,448	$13,344,140	98%
MA	$55,622,122	$106,700,567	92%
CT	$64,468,941	$122,054,807	89%

* Includes only those states where industry members
remitted more than $5 million in FET in FY 2013

- TTB will continue its current enforcement activities in FY 2014 and expand its enforcement initiatives to include other points in the supply chain that are at risk for diversion activity. According to TTB data, non-taxpaid removals of alcohol and tobacco products from bonded premises have an excise tax exposure of about $380 million and $1 billion annually, respectively. Alcohol and tobacco products intended for export and removed from a TTB-licensed manufacturer to a customs bonded warehouse, foreign trade zone, or tobacco export warehouse may be diverted illegally into U.S. commerce without tax payment. In FY 2013, TTB piloted its forward trace investigations on high-risk tobacco export warehouses that resulted in numerous findings of tax-free cigarettes being diverted back into U.S. commerce. TTB is initiating tax assessments that total over $3.2 million based on the diversion activity identified in FY 2013, and will also take appropriate permit action against the companies engaged in the illicit activity. In partnership with CBP, TTB will continue to expand its proven intelligence and investigative techniques to make significant inroads into identifying tax evasion schemes that involve the diversion of non-taxpaid products intended for export.

- The complexity of criminal diversion cases requires leveraging all of TTB's enforcement resources to identify, investigate, and successfully prosecute offenders. In FY 2013, TTB continued its team-based enforcement approach for major criminal cases with potential nationwide impact. TTB's National Response Teams completed successful civil examinations and referred several criminal cases, identifying over $17.3 million in potential federal excise tax liabilities.

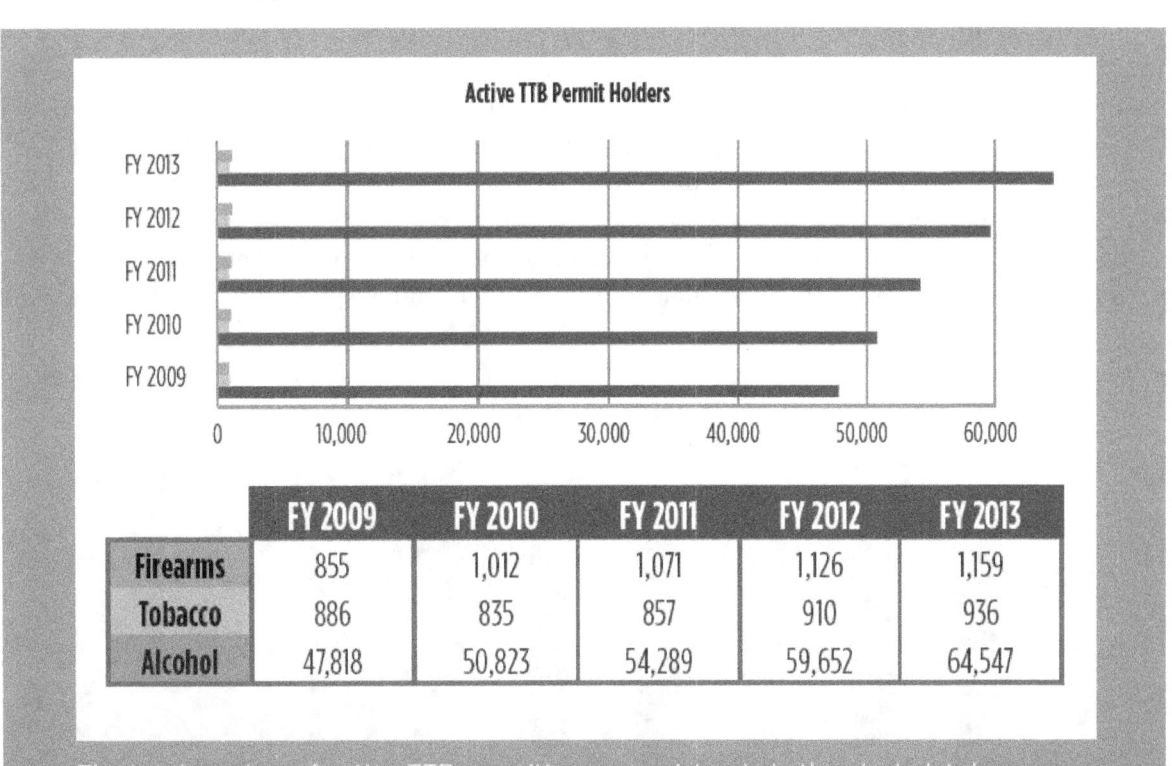

	FY 2009	FY 2010	FY 2011	FY 2012	FY 2013
Firearms	855	1,012	1,071	1,126	1,159
Tobacco	886	835	857	910	936
Alcohol	47,818	50,823	54,289	59,652	64,547

The total number of active TTB permittees or registrants in the alcohol, tobacco, and firearms industries has increased 34 percent since FY 2009. Since last year, the number has grown another 8 percent. Alcohol manufacturers, importers, and wholesalers comprise the vast majority of TTB permittees, or approximately 97 percent. Tobacco permittees and firearms registrants also trended up slightly, with a 3 percent increase compared to FY 2012.

Protect the Public

TTB met all but one of its performance measures under the *Protect the Public* activity. A detailed summary of TTB performance is discussed in Part II of this report, Program Performance Results.

Investments in the Protect the Public mission resulted in several key achievements during FY 2013:

Permitting of Alcohol and Tobacco Businesses

- TTB facilitates commerce by permitting businesses engaged in the alcohol and tobacco industries. In FY 2013, TTB processed more than 7,700 applications for a federal permit, and issued an original permit to approximately 5,900 start-up businesses. The number of permits processed is down slightly compared to 2012, but remains approximately 20 percent above the five-year average. The Permits Online system has helped TTB manage the influx of applications resulting from sustained growth in its regulated industries. However, improvements to processing times that TTB anticipates from ongoing system enhancements and other efficacy measures may not materialize until these efforts are completed in FY 2015. In FY 2013, processing times increased by 17 percent from 69 days in FY 2012 to 81 days in FY 2013.

- As illicit activity in the alcohol and tobacco industries has the potential to be highly lucrative, it is crucial that TTB investigate permit applicants to prevent criminal operatives from obtaining a permit to engage in the alcohol and tobacco trade. In support of this objective, TTB initiated approximately 275 permit investigations to verify that applicants were qualified and not prohibited from engaging in business activity in the alcohol and tobacco industries, and that those operating in these industries were properly permitted and operating in compliance with federal regulations. TTB also performs post-application investigations to verify that those who were issued a permit in the prior year supplied accurate information on their application and are conducting compliant operations. In the instances where an industry member provided false information or had significant compliance violations, TTB took appropriate corrective action, including the surrender, suspension, or revocation of the industry member's permit.

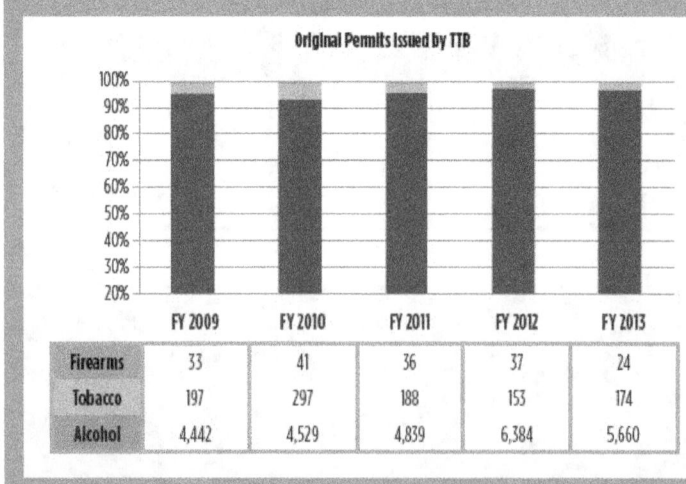

In five years, the total number of original permits and registrations approved by TTB has grown 25 percent. Alcohol wholesaler permits spiked in FY 2012 due to a change in Washington State law, and have since decreased. Total permits and registrations issued remains 8 percent above the five-year average. Firearms registrations approved by TTB decreased, while the number of tobacco permits issued trended up due to an increase in the number of manufacturers of processed tobacco.

Alcohol Beverage Label Approval

- A Certificate of Label Approval (COLA) is required before a manufacturer or importer of alcohol beverages can introduce their product into interstate commerce. In FY 2013, TTB processed more than 140,000 COLA applications, with approximately 85 percent obtaining TTB approval.

- After a decade of nearly constant annual growth, TTB was effective in implementing policy changes to reverse the upward trend in label submissions, enabling TTB to better respond to the demand for TTB services. By revising the label application form to expand the list of items that may be changed on an alcohol beverage label without TTB pre-approval, TTB reduced the number of new and resubmitted label applications by 8 percent in FY 2013. Going forward, TTB will continue to look for similar solutions to reduce regulatory burden and help industry members get their products to the marketplace faster without compromising its statutory mandates to ensure alcohol beverages are truthfully and accurately labeled.

- Electronic filing rates for COLA applications continue to increase, with 92 percent of applications submitted through COLAs Online, the Bureau's system for the electronic filing of label applications. TTB was successful in increasing the rate of e-filing by 1 percent over the previous fiscal year and in reaching and sustaining its long-term target of a 90 percent electronic filing rate. Incremental improvements in the years ahead will be achieved through improvements to online information and system demonstrations targeted toward the highest volume paper filers.

- Obtaining label approval for certain alcohol products also requires TTB approval of the formula for that product. TTB reviews alcohol beverage formulas to verify that the products are appropriately labeled and do not pose a risk to consumer safety. TTB's review of formulas also serves a tax purpose, as the tax rate on alcohol beverages may change depending on the product formulation. Formula submissions have skyrocketed in recent years, largely due to rapid industry growth, particularly among craft brewers and distillers. Since 2009, formula submissions have more than doubled, totaling over 12,500 in FY 2013. The

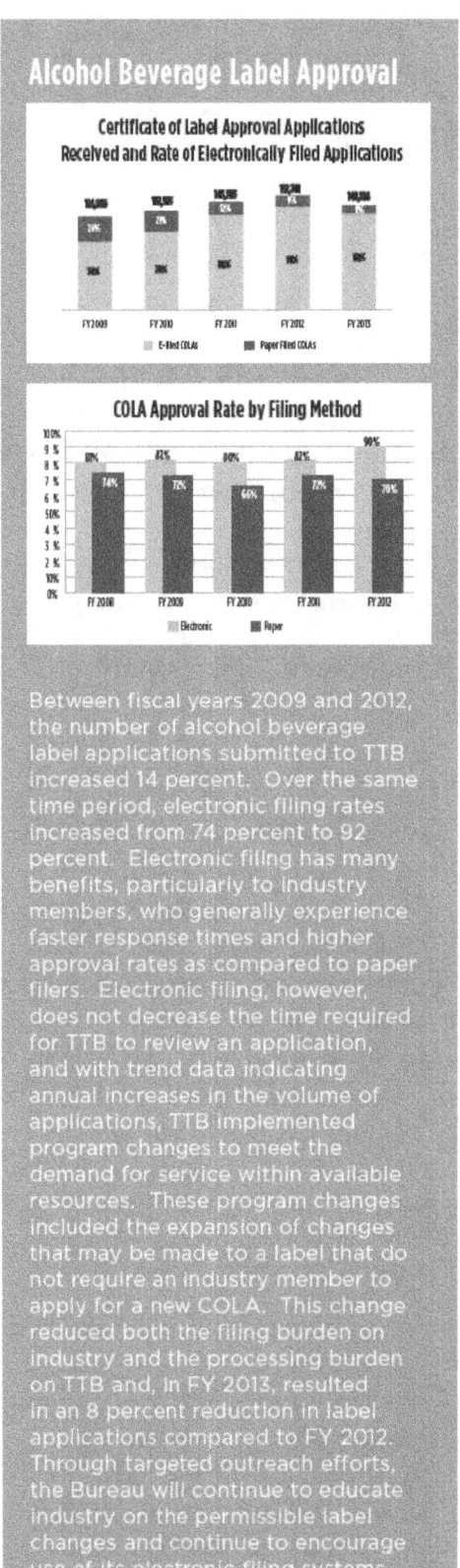

Alcohol Beverage Label Approval

Certificate of Label Approval Applications Received and Rate of Electronically Filed Applications

COLA Approval Rate by Filing Method

Between fiscal years 2009 and 2012, the number of alcohol beverage label applications submitted to TTB increased 14 percent. Over the same time period, electronic filing rates increased from 74 percent to 92 percent. Electronic filing has many benefits, particularly to industry members, who generally experience faster response times and higher approval rates as compared to paper filers. Electronic filing, however, does not decrease the time required for TTB to review an application, and with trend data indicating annual increases in the volume of applications, TTB implemented program changes to meet the demand for service within available resources. These program changes included the expansion of changes that may be made to a label that do not require an industry member to apply for a new COLA. This change reduced both the filing burden on industry and the processing burden on TTB and, in FY 2013, resulted in an 8 percent reduction in label applications compared to FY 2012. Through targeted outreach efforts, the Bureau will continue to educate industry on the permissible label changes and continue to encourage use of its electronic filing systems.

combination of increased submissions and reduced resources resulted in processing times for formula approvals rising by 176 percent to an average of 47 days. As a formula approval must be obtained before TTB can issue a COLA, the cumulative wait time in FY 2013 for formula and label approval averaged more than two and a half months. Addressing these challenges is critical to facilitating vibrant, compliant trade. TTB continues to evaluate the current formula requirements to determine whether certain requirements are no longer necessary or if the submission and review process could be streamlined.

- Since the release of Formulas Online in January 2011, the rate of electronically filed formula applications has continued to increase each year. From an initial e-filing rate of 23 percent, TTB now receives 73 percent of its formula applications for beverage alcohol products electronically. Additionally, approximately 65 percent of nonbeverage alcohol producers submit formula applications electronically to TTB. TTB marketed Formulas Online in several significant ways in FY 2013. TTB conducted Formulas Online Improvement Forums with representatives and members of the alcohol beverage industry. TTB also delivered webinars to promote the use of Formulas Online for non-beverage formula applications. These webinars were targeted to increase system use by flavor manufacturers, special denatured alcohol producers, and dietary supplement manufacturers.

Marketplace Enforcement of Label Compliance

- In assuring the integrity of alcohol beverage products offered for sale to U.S. consumers, TTB conducts marketplace sampling to ensure that product labels contain adequate descriptive information and that products do not contain ingredients that will harm consumers. TTB's Alcohol Beverage Sampling Program (ABSP) is a random survey of wine, distilled spirits, and malt beverage products in the marketplace to determine where compliance issues exist and proactively respond to potential labeling issues or threats to the food supply. In cases when technical analysis of the label and bottle contents identifies a compliance issue, TTB notifies the industry member about the violation and works with them to bring the product into compliance, with field investigations initiated for significant violations. Significant violations that required investigation in FY 2013 included wines that were misclassified for tax purposes and a case involving possible COLA fraud. Further, ABSP results in recent years indicate that proofing and gauging of distilled spirits is a recurring compliance issue. Because the excise tax for distilled spirits is based on alcohol content, proper gauging of distilled spirits is vital in proper tax determination. To address this issue, TTB is developing educational tools to assist distillers with their gauging skills. For a full report on the FY 2013 ABSP findings, please visit TTB.gov.

Product Safety and Testing

- In FY 2013, as part of its program to ensure the safety of alcohol beverages, TTB responded to several instances of adulterated or contaminated alcohol beverage products. These instances included coordinating a response to a Chinese spirits product with high levels of phthalates, a synthetic chemical that may be linked to adverse developmental and reproductive effects; overseeing the voluntary recall of a distilled spirits specialty product that did not have the required sulfite warning, a required allergen disclosure; and overseeing the voluntary recall of a gin product that contained glass particles. TTB works in partnership with the U.S. Food and Drug Administration (FDA) to address potential health hazards related to alcohol beverage products, as TTB considers an adulterated alcohol beverage product, as defined by the Federal Food, Drug, and Cosmetic Act and determined by the FDA, to be mislabeled under federal alcohol beverage labeling laws.

- TTB laboratories continuously develop new capabilities to support TTB's consumer protection mission. TTB currently allows voluntary allergen labeling for alcohol beverages; however, current testing methods for detecting allergens in alcohol beverages is often inadequate. TTB is developing a secondary method that may be used in conjunction with the current testing technique to detect and quantify egg and milk proteins in wine. TTB worked closely with the Wine Institute's Technical Committee and FDA's Center for Food Safety and Applied Nutrition to obtain test samples and identify chemical markers to support this effort.

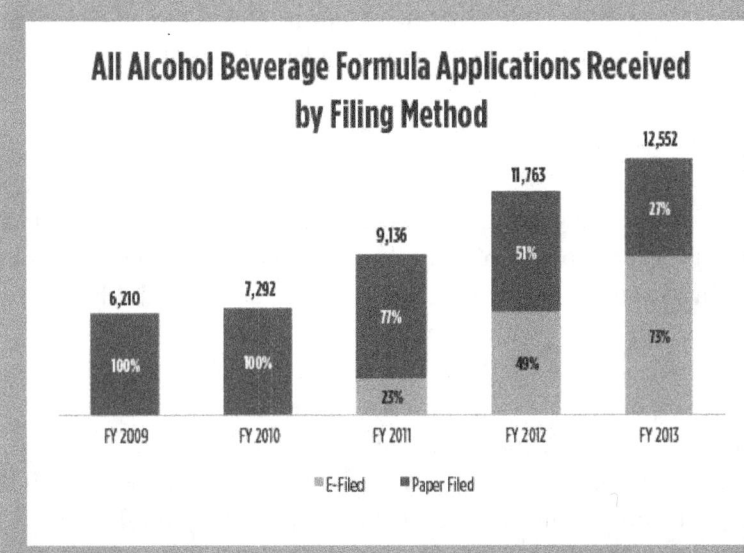

The total number of beverage formula applications includes distilled spirits, malt beverage, wine, and pre-import and laboratory analyses.

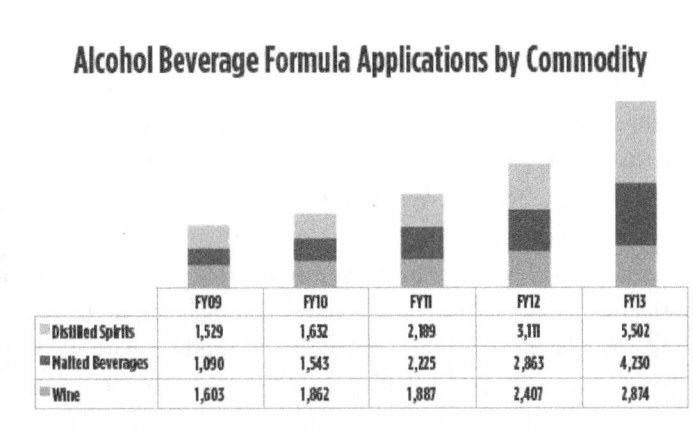

	FY09	FY10	FY11	FY12	FY13
Distilled Spirits	1,529	1,632	2,189	3,111	5,502
Malted Beverages	1,090	1,543	2,225	2,863	4,230
Wine	1,603	1,862	1,887	2,407	2,874

In five years, the total number of alcohol beverage formulas applications has grown 102 percent. Product innovation and the growth in the number of craft brewers and distillers has contributed to the overall increase in formula submissions. The majority of formula submissions are for distilled spirits products (e.g., flavored vodkas, liqueurs) and non-traditional malt beverages (e.g., flavored malt beverages, beers made with fruit, spices, or other flavorings). There are also formula requirements for certain types of wines.

Following a year of nearly 30 percent growth, formula applications increased another 7 percent in FY 2013. Efficiencies gained from the Formulas Online electronic filing system, which TTB launched in 2011, do not offset the significant increase in the volume of submissions. TTB continues to evaluate broader changes to its formulation requirements to reflect modern industry practices and consumer interests, and which have the potential to reduce the volume of submissions that industry must submit and TTB must pre-approve.

Trade Practice Enforcement

- As part of its Trade Facilitation Program, TTB investigates acts that violate federal law relating to alcohol beverage trade practices. Trade practice violations undermine fair competition within the trade and, thus, artificially influence consumer access to products based upon anti-competitive practices by influential producers. One such prohibited marketing practice, called "tied-house," makes it unlawful for an industry member to induce any retailer to purchase its alcohol beverage products to the exclusion of other products or industry members. In FY 2013, TTB initiated a market survey to evaluate the use of shelf plans and schematics given by industry members to retailers. TTB followed the market survey with a national investigation pertaining to shelf schematics and shelf management programs. During the investigation, TTB determined that it is standard practice for industry members who provide shelf plans and shelf schematics to retailers to also provide shelf space management services. Providing such services is considered "a thing of value" under the FAA Act, and thus an unlawful inducement. TTB is currently considering various options to address this nation-wide issue.

International Trade Facilitation

- TTB's Trade Facilitation program also helps to strengthen the U.S. economy by facilitating import and export trade in alcohol beverage products, while also administering the consumer protection standards under TTB's jurisdiction. The Bureau has made significant progress in recent years in establishing and effectively employing its international agreements with counterpart agencies in countries that are among the United States' top trading partners. In FY 2013, TTB signed a memorandum of understanding with the Wine Australia Corporation (Wine Australia). Wine Australia is responsible for export regulation and compliance, wine sector information and analysis, and assisting in negotiations with other countries to reduce trade barriers. Wine Australia is a key counterpart for TTB as Australia is the third-largest source of imported wine in the United States (after Italy and France), accounting for 14 percent of wine imports in 2010. These agreements are designed to facilitate trade by increasing mutual understanding of each country's alcohol and tobacco production requirements and labeling and licensing standards, and provide a process for the exchange of regulatory information that has the potential to enhance protection of the revenue or impact product trade, compliance, and safety.

- As the U.S. tax and regulatory authority for alcohol beverages, TTB must issue certificates for U.S. producers in order for the producers to be able to export their products to many foreign countries. In FY 2013, TTB issued more than 15,000 export certificates for beer, wine, and distilled spirits. Without these certificates, which are only issued by TTB, U.S. producers of alcohol beverages cannot sell their products in certain major markets abroad. Through its international outreach, TTB has arranged for the elimination or reduction of certification requirements for wine exported to various countries, with significant progress made in FY 2013 to streamline requirements of Chinese regulatory agencies. Currently, United States exporters send four separate certificates with each shipment to meet China's importation rules, including certificates of free sale, origin, health, and sanitation. To streamline the certification and clearance process, in FY 2012, TTB proposed to Chinese authorities the use of a consolidated wine export certificate. In June 2013, TTB and the Chinese authorities reached agreement on the content of the consolidated certificate. TTB will announce the date when the consolidated certificate will be accepted at Chinese ports.

- TTB continued its coordination with wine regulators from the economies of the Asia-Pacific Economic Cooperation (APEC). APEC is the premier forum for facilitating economic growth, cooperation, trade, and investment in the Asia-Pacific region, and the 21 member countries are emerging export markets for the U.S. wine industry. In FY 2013, APEC announced its approval of a multi-year project proposal for work on wine issues. The United States and 11 co-sponsoring economies submitted the proposal to APEC to enhance trade through the spread of good regulatory practices and improved regulatory capabilities across APEC. The proposal includes activities related to wine certification, technical workshops, information exchanges, and collaboration on international standards. The first major activity of the multi-year project will be a technical workshop in Washington, D.C., in early FY 2014.

- TTB works to address barriers of trade in the international marketplace by supporting the United States Trade Representative (USTR) in the negotiation of international trade agreements related to alcohol and tobacco products. In FY 2013, TTB provided technical expertise to USTR for the negotiation of the Trans-Pacific Partnership Agreement (TPP). The TPP—a free-trade agreement being negotiated between Australia, Brunei, Canada, Chile, Japan, Malaysia, Mexico, New Zealand, Peru, Singapore, the United States, and Vietnam—includes a Wine and Spirits Annex in the chapter on technical barriers to trade. The Annex aims to reduce trade barriers in the regulation of wine and spirits by defining acceptable procedures in the areas of labeling, identity standards, conformity assessments, compliance periods, and acceptance of oenological practices.

- In FY 2013, TTB participated in two bilateral meetings with representatives of the European Commission relating to the United States-European Union (EU) Agreement on Trade in Wine. The EU is the top export market for U.S. wine, and is the largest source of imported wine in the United States. Maintaining a free flow of trade between the two economies is vital to U.S. economic growth. The meetings covered trade issues including organic wine standards, certifications for U.S. wine shipments, the use of certain "traditional terms" (e.g., chateau, clos, ruby, and tawny) on labels of U.S. wine exported to the EU, and allergen statements. Also in FY 2013, the U.S. and EU announced the start of negotiations on a comprehensive free trade agreement between the two economies, known as the Transatlantic Trade and Investment Partnership (TTIP). TTB will continue to provide technical assistance to the U.S. TTIP delegation regarding alcohol beverage issues, including intellectual property issues, agricultural market access, and technical barriers to trade, and will work to ensure the protection of U.S. stakeholders' interests.

American Viticultural Areas

An American Viticultural Area (AVA) is a delimited grape-growing region having a viticulturally significant name, a delineated boundary, and distinguishing features as described in part 9 of the TTB regulations. Distinguishing features may include climate, geology, soils, physical features, and elevation.

An AVA designation allows vintners and consumers to attribute a quality, reputation, or other characteristic of a wine made from grapes grown in an area to its geographic region. The establishment of an AVA allows vintners to more accurately describe the origin of their wines to consumers and helps consumers to identify wines that they may purchase.

TTB published 11 AVA-related documents in FY 2013. Three of those documents established new AVAs, the Ancient Lakes of Columbia Valley AVA, the Indiana Uplands AVA, and the Elkton Oregon AVA. Additionally, TTB proposed the establishment of the Ballard Canyon AVA, the Moon Mountain District Sonoma County AVA, the Big Valley-Lake County AVA, the Kelsey Bench-Lake County AVA, the Malibu Coast AVA, the Upper Hiawassee Highlands AVA, and the Eagle Peak-Mendocino County AVA.

Aerial photograph depicting the boundary lines of the proposed Ballard Canyon American Viticulture Area. The Ballard Canyon AVA encompasses 7,800 acres in Santa Barbara County, California.

TTB also published a notice of proposed rulemaking that proposed the establishment of 11 new AVAs within the already existing Paso Robles AVA in San Luis Obispo County, California. The 11 proposed AVAs include the Adelaida District AVA, the Creston District AVA, the El Pomar District AVA, the Paso Robles Estrella District AVA, the Paso Robles Geneseo District AVA, the Paso Robles Highlands District AVA, the Paso Robles Willow Creek District AVA, the San Juan Creek AVA, the San Miguel District AVA, the Santa Margarita Ranch AVA, and the Templeton Gap District AVA.

At the end of FY 2013, TTB and its predecessor agency, the Bureau of Alcohol, Tobacco and Firearms, had established a total of 208 AVAs.

Financial Summary

Federal Excise Tax Collections

TTB collects excise taxes from the alcohol, tobacco, firearms, and ammunition industries. In addition, the Bureau collects Special Occupational Tax (SOT) from certain tobacco businesses. During FY 2013, TTB collected $22.9 billion in taxes, interest, and other revenues.

Substantially all of the taxes collected by TTB are remitted to the Department of the Treasury General Fund. The firearms and ammunition excise taxes (FAET) are an exception. This revenue is remitted to the Fish and Wildlife Restoration Fund under provisions of the Pittman-Robertson Act of 1937. The U.S. Fish and Wildlife Service, which oversees the fund, apportions the money to State governments for wildlife restoration and research, and hunter education programs.

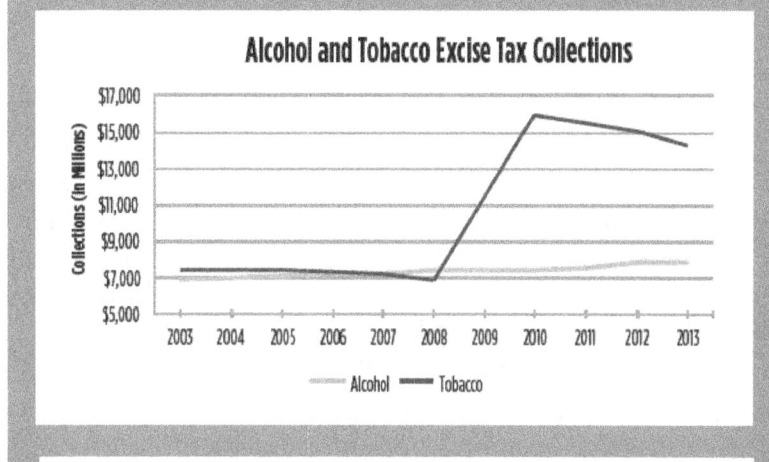

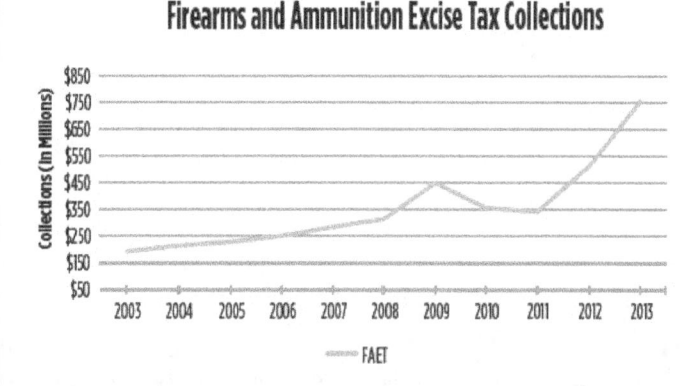

TTB's tax collections for domestic alcohol beverages have shown a relatively stable rising trend for several years. The tax for imported alcohol beverages is collected by U.S. Customs and Border Protection.

Tobacco tax revenues in FY 2013 decreased by 4.5 percent from the prior year. This trend tracks with Congressional Budget Office projections for tobacco tax revenue following the passage of the CHIPRA legislation.

FAET revenues continue to rise, with total collections up 48 percent compared to the prior year. Since TTB assumed the responsibility for administering the FAET in 2003, collections have increased 294 percent.

FY 2013 Excise Tax Collections:	
Alcohol	$7,851,953,000
Tobacco	$14,321,017,000
FAET	$762,836,000
SOT	$280,000
FST	$1,521,000
Other	$38,000
Total	$22,937,645,000

Refunds and Other Payments

During FY 2013, TTB issued $739 million in tax refunds, cover-over payments, and drawback payments on taxes paid by manufacturers of nonbeverage products (MNBPs).

Cover-over Payments

Federal excise taxes are collected under the Internal Revenue Code of 1986 on certain articles produced in Puerto Rico and the U.S. Virgin Islands (USVI) that are brought or imported into the United States. In accordance with 26 U.S.C. 7652, such taxes collected on rum imported into the U.S. are "covered over," or paid into the treasuries of Puerto Rico and USVI, less the collection expenses incurred by TTB. TTB also issues cover-over payments to Puerto Rico and USVI for "other Caribbean rum," which is the rum imported into the United States from other countries or other U.S. possessions.[14] During FY 2013, cover-over payments totaled $358 million, with $349 million paid to Puerto Rico and $9 million paid to USVI[15] for their proportional share of all Caribbean rum tax collections. Year-to-year, cover-over payments can vary depending on the rate of payments, which is established by statute.

Drawback Payments

Under current law (26 U.S.C. 5134), MNBPs may be eligible to claim a refund of taxes paid on distilled spirits used in their products. During FY 2013, drawback payments totaled $345 million.

For distilled spirits on which the tax has been paid or determined, a drawback is allowed on each proof gallon at the rate of $1 less than the rate at which the distilled spirits tax had been paid or determined. The refund is due upon the claimant providing evidence that the distilled spirits on which the tax has been paid or determined is unfit for beverage purposes or was used in the manufacture of medicines, medicinal preparations, food products, flavors, flavoring extracts, or perfume. The claimant must submit a product formula to the TTB laboratory for analysis and approval of the nonbeverage claim. To assess drawback claims, the TTB laboratory analyzed approximately 10,000 formulas and samples in FY 2013.

FY 2013 Excise Tax Refunds:	
Alcohol and Tobacco Excise Tax Refunds	$35,278,000
Cover-over Payments, Puerto Rico	$349,017,000
Cover-over Payments, Virgin Islands	$8,706,000
Drawbacks on MNBP Claims	$345,231,000
Interest and Other Payments	$452,000
Total	$738,684,000

14 The cover-over payments made to Puerto Rico and the Virgin Islands based on taxes collected on "other Caribbean rum" is distributed between the territories based on a formula set forth in 27 CFR 26.31.

15 The Department of the Interior also issues cover-over payments to USVI under Public Law 95-348.

FY 2013 Bureau Budget

Direct Appropriations (Salaries & Expense Account)

TTB's budget authority under the 2013 Full-Year Continuing Appropriations Act was $99,878,000, less the sequestration reduction ($5,024,463) and the across-the-board rescission ($199,756), decreasing TTB's FY 2013 budget to $94,653,781. This amount included $1,895,388 for the costs of special law enforcement agents to target tobacco smuggling and other criminal diversion activities. TTB elected not to hire the agents directly, but to enter into an interagency agreement with the Internal Revenue Service Criminal Investigation office to conduct criminal investigations into violations of the tax laws TTB enforces. The FY 2013 President's Budget authorized 482 full-time equivalent (FTE) positions for TTB.

Reimbursable Authority

During FY 2013, the Bureau realized reimbursable authority in the amount of $5.9 million. Those funds originated from multiple sources, including recoveries from the operation of the cover-over program and other enforcement activities in Puerto Rico ($3.1 million); funding from the Department of the Treasury's Executive Office of Asset Forfeiture to cover investigative expenses ($300 thousand); and reimbursement from the Community Development Financial Institutions Fund (CDFI) ($2.5 million) for information technology support services.

Sequestration

As with most of the federal government, TTB's 2013 budget was affected by the broad automatic spending cuts resulting from the Budget Control Act of 2011 (BCA), which were generally referred to as sequestration. These spending cuts were initially scheduled to begin on January 1, 2013, but were postponed for two months by the American Taxpayer Relief Act of 2012. The sequestration discretionary spending caps took effect on March 1, resulting in a TTB budget reduction of $5,024,463 (including a rescission cut of $199,756), representing a 5.2 percent decrease in TTB's annual appropriation.

The Bureau achieved these reductions through a series of cuts to three principal budget cost components: 1) TTB's staffing level (a 4 percent reduction of TTB's government workforce); 2) contract support; and 3) operating costs. The cumulative impact of these reductions, combined with other budget reductions sustained in recent years, resulted in a number of consequences relating to the Bureau's ability to achieve its mission, including increases in permit and label application processing times, which adversely affect tax revenue and the overall economy. Without a federal permit, businesses cannot manufacture alcohol and tobacco products, and therefore would not pay taxes on goods that they would have manufactured. Similarly, because TTB collects the tax on alcohol beverage products at the point of removal from an industry member's premises, delays in label application processing affects tax collections.

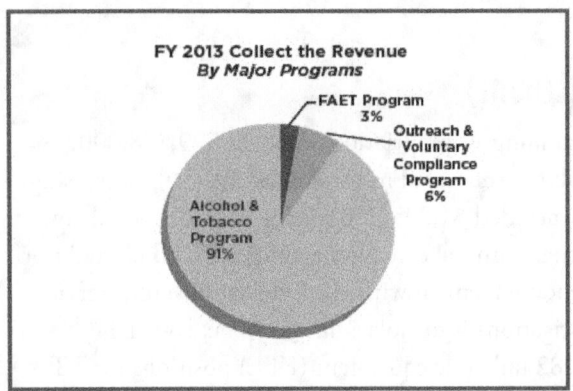
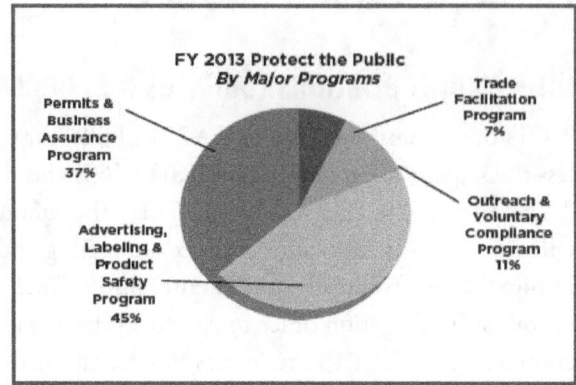

The Bureau's expenditures by its major programs remained relatively consistent between fiscal years 2012 and 2013.

Audit of TTB's FY 2013 Financial Statements

The Department of the Treasury is one of 23 federal agencies that are required by law to produce annual audited financial statements. TTB's financial activities are an integral part of the information reported on by the Treasury Department.

TTB's Annual Report includes audited FY 2012 and FY 2013 financial statements; the Independent Auditors' Report addresses these financial statements and reports on the Bureau's internal controls over financial reporting and compliance with laws and regulations.

Management Assurances

An independent, full-scope financial statement audit was conducted for FY 2013 and TTB received an unmodified audit opinion. For FY 2013, TTB provides reasonable assurance that the objectives of the Federal Managers' Financial Integrity Act have been achieved, and the Bureau's financial management systems are in substantial compliance with the Federal Financial Management Improvement Act. This overall determination is based on past and current practices, an improved controls environment, scrutiny by external audit sources, internal evaluations, and administrative and fiscal accounting system enhancements.

During FY 2013, TTB also applied its custom risk management tools to its Revenue Accounting Section to identify risks in the accounting and tracking of TTB's annual federal excise tax collections and to the National Revenue Center, with a focus on its key business processes. Based on these tools, TTB has adequate internal controls in place to mitigate risk to operations, and the overall risk of fraud, waste, and abuse is "LOW."

Bureau Challenges

TTB plans to revisit the vulnerability and risk management tools that are used each year to monitor the internal controls over tax collections to ensure these documents reflect the key business processes in operation at the National Revenue Center and fully support our internal control program at the Bureau. As systems and businesses processes change, it is important that TTB update the tools used to monitor its tax processing activities.

Part II:
Program Performance Results

Performance Overview

TTB reports its performance in terms of five metrics that represent its ability to foster compliance from taxpayers, employ technology to meet its public protection mission, and return value to the Nation for the investment in TTB programs.

TTB exceeded the performance targets for four of the five measures reported to its stakeholders in FY 2013. TTB achieved 75 percent of its targeted performance level for the measure that it did not meet. Based on external factors and the results achieved this fiscal year, TTB reviewed its FY 2014 performance targets and set targets that reflect workload projections, resource constraints, planned business process improvements, and anticipated impacts from technology enhancements. To meet its performance goals in FY 2014, TTB will implement an aggressive strategic agenda that integrates new technology, human capital management strategies, and targeted efforts in both outreach and enforcement. All performance results are subject to management review and periodic audit by the Department of the Treasury.

FY 2013 Performance Measure Status	
Performance Targets Met	4
Performance Targets Not Met	1
Baseline	0
Total Performance Measures	5

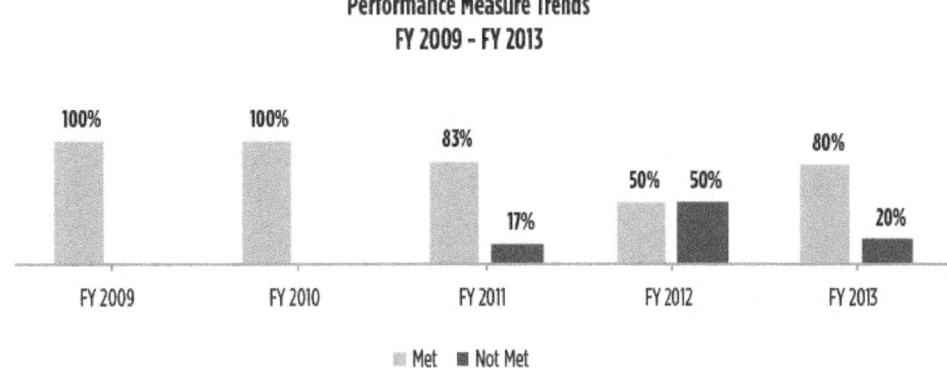

Performance Measure Trends
FY 2009 - FY 2013

FY 2009	FY 2010	FY 2011	FY 2012	FY 2013
100%	100%	83% / 17%	50% / 50%	80% / 20%

■ Met ■ Not Met

*In FY 2012, TTB met 50 percent of its performance targets as opposed to the 67 percent reported last year. The error was due to the discontinuation of TTB's customer survey measure in FY 2012.

Performance Measure	FY 09 Actual	FY 10 Actual	FY 11 Actual	FY 12 Actual	FY 13 Target	FY 13 Actual	FY 14 Target	FY 13 Target Met?	% of Target Reached
Amount of revenue collected per program dollar	$427	$478	$468	$449	$400	**$457**	$400	Y	114%
Percentage of voluntary compliance from large taxpayers in filing timely tax payments (in terms of revenue)	94%	94%	95%	92%	90%	**92%**	91%	Y	102%

Performance Discussion

In FY 2013, TTB met both of its annual targets for the performance measures under the Collect the Revenue budget activity. Taken together, TTB's measures of the Amount of Revenue Collected per Program Dollar and the Percent of Voluntary Compliance from Large Taxpayers in Filing Payments Timely demonstrate the effectiveness and efficiency with which TTB operates its revenue collection mission. Achieving results for both measures was supported by the proactive application of technology to streamline internal and external processes and an effective tax enforcement presence that leveraged both real-time intelligence data and interagency partnerships with counterpart enforcement agencies.

Improve Efficiency of Tax Collection

The Amount of Revenue Collected per Program Dollar measure uses annual collections figures and the actual expenditures and obligations for collection activities to quantify the efficiency of TTB's tax collection program. In FY 2013, TTB collected nearly $23 billion in excise taxes and other revenues from approximately 9,300 taxpayers in the alcohol, tobacco, firearms, and ammunition industries.

The return on investment for TTB's tax collection activities consistently exceeds 400:1 and, in FY 2013, reached 457:1. Effective enforcement combined with process improvements and streamlining efforts should contribute to continued positive returns on the investment in TTB.

In setting its annual performance targets, TTB examines historical collections trends across each of its regulated commodities, as well as other predictors that influence consumer behaviors. Specifically, shifts in consumption patterns, product manufacturing, and trade will impact federal revenues in the years ahead. In accounting for these types of marketplace shifts, TTB used Congressional Budget Office revenue projections for tobacco excise tax collections to determine the targeted performance level of 400:1 for fiscal years 2014 – 2015.

Excise Tax and Other Collections by Fiscal Year

(Dollars in Thousands)

Fiscal Year	Alcohol	Tobacco	FAET	SOT	FST	Other	Total
2004	$6,995,366	$7,433,852	$216,006	$100,562	$-	$359	$14,746,145
2005	7,074,076	7,409,608	225,818	10,190	9	141	14,719,842
2006	7,182,940	7,350,058	249,578	2,895	638	146	14,786,255
2007	7,232,138	7,194,081	287,835	2,808	-	32	14,716,894
2008	7,420,576	6,851,705	312,622	448	-	634	14,585,985
2009	7,424,292	11,548,504	452,693	272	1,192,375	970	20,619,106
2010	7,476,789	15,913,479	360,813	300	8,558	180	23,760,119
2011	7,594,330	15,515,073	344,262	268	5,220	2,257	23,461,410
2012	7,856,391	15,002,616	514,622	249	5,942	61	23,379,881
2013	7,851,953	14,321,017	762,836	280	1,521	38	22,937,645
Average	$7,410,885	$10,853,999	$372,709	$11,827	$121,426	$482	$18,771,328

FAET - Firearms and Ammunition Excise Tax   SOT - Special Occupational Tax   FST - Floor Stock Tax   Other - Suspense Account

To meet its FY 2014 performance target of $400, TTB will continue to improve efficiencies and results in its tax enforcement program by improving the systems and processes related to tax verification. On the front end, TTB will implement plans to increase automation in the detection, notification, assessment, and collection of excise taxes to preserve staff time for substantive tax analysis. On the back end, TTB will continue to develop and build risk models based on multiple data sources to identify high-risk activity or high-risk taxpayers for audit and investigation. Continuous refinements to these models and sound intelligence enable TTB to efficiently deploy its limited enforcement resources. A primary focus for TTB tax enforcement continues to be tobacco manufacturers and importers, including importers of processed tobacco. Transfers of this non-taxpaid tobacco product carry a high revenue risk, as the product may be diverted for illicit cigarette manufacturing. TTB's investigations in this area have resulted in multiple civil and criminal cases that have identified more than $180 million in potential revenue loss from the diversion of more than 10 million pounds of processed tobacco to non-permitted entities. TTB will continue these and other priority enforcement initiatives related to on the import and export trade of alcohol and tobacco products in FY 2014, successfully combining data analytics with advanced field investigative techniques to detect and address tax evasion.

Increase Voluntary Compliance from Taxpayers

Fostering voluntary compliance among excise taxpayers is a primary tax administration strategy for TTB. The Percent of Voluntary Compliance from Large Taxpayers in Filing Tax Payments Timely is a key performance metric that shows the rate of compliance by large taxpayers (i.e., those that pay more than $50,000 in annual taxes) in voluntarily filing their tax payments on or before the scheduled due date. After a drop in the compliance rate in FY 2012, TTB set a performance target of 90 percent in FY 2013; at year-end, TTB achieved a 92 percent rate of compliance from its large taxpayers. The voluntary compliance rate continues to be significantly lower in the latter half of the year as efforts to enforce tax compliance result in the submission of additional late filings by TTB taxpayers. Perhaps counter intuitively, improvements in the Bureau's ability to detect non-compliance due to the effective deployment of its automated tool for the identification of late, missing, and errant tax returns and operational reports has caused a temporary decrease in in this performance metric. As TTB continues to enhance the functionality of this automated tool, TTB expects that its reported compliance rate for timely filings may continue to decline in the short term before these enforcement efforts lead to demonstrable improvements in industry compliance.

TTB expects to meet its FY 2014 performance target of a 91 percent voluntary compliance rate for its large taxpayers. During a period of economic recovery, TTB believes that this is an aggressive target for taxpayer compliance and will demonstrate the effectiveness of TTB's strategies to improve industry understanding of and compliance with federal tax requirements. TTB will employ complementary strategies to meet its performance target that focus on enhancing electronic filing options to enable taxpayers to file complete, accurate, and timely tax returns and payments; improving online guidance, particularly for the large number of newly permitted industry members; and maintaining an enforcement presence to encourage voluntary compliance. Moving forward on all three fronts will ensure that TTB strikes the appropriate balance between supporting new businesses in setting up compliant operations while ensuring adequate coverage of the high-risk activity that undermines lawful business activity.

Electronic Filing Improvements

Beginning now and continuing into FY 2015, TTB will intensify its efforts to increase the electronic filing rate of its taxpayers. TTB expanded its e-filing program to allow all excise taxpayers to file required tax returns, reports, and payments online through the Pay.gov system, with approximately 23 percent of excise tax returns and 34 percent of operational reports submitted electronically through Pay.gov in FY 2013. As part of a comprehensive strategy to promote e-filing by TTB taxpayers, TTB plans to address a primary hindrance for industry members in using Pay.gov by enabling the system to accept credit card payments. This enhancement would also address a timing issue that requires those who file electronically to remit tax payments early. TTB is partnering with the Bureau of the Fiscal Service in this effort, which supports the Department of the Treasury's Agency Priority Goals related to improving voluntary tax compliance and increasing paperless transactions.

Industry Education and Outreach

TTB is planning a series of online initiatives for FY 2014 to improve guidance, transparency, and collaboration between TTB and industry. Given the increase in new industry members, TTB will provide online training and Webinars to ensure that these taxpayers understand and are able to comply with the applicable federal tax and regulatory requirements. These activities will promote compliance across the regulated industries and support TTB's achievement of its FY 2014 performance target.

Criminal Enforcement

As an identifiable enforcement presence is a well-established driver of compliance rates, TTB expects to achieve higher rates of voluntary compliance as the Bureau expands its enforcement initiatives. TTB will continue to establish a visible enforcement presence that includes special agents to address the revenue threat posed by alcohol and tobacco diversion and to ensure that compliant businesses are not competing against illegitimate competitors that are producing non-taxpaid products.

Performance Measure	FY 09 Actual	FY 10 Actual	FY 11 Actual	FY 12 Actual	FY 13 Target	FY 13 Actual	FY 14 Target	FY 13 Target Met?	% of Target Reached
Percent of electronically filed Certificate of Label Approval (COLA) applications	74%	79%	88%	91%	92%	**92%**	93%	Y	100%
National Revenue Center (NRC) customer service survey results	89%	89%	90%	84%	DISC	DISC	DISC		
Average number of days to process an original permit application for a new alcohol or tobacco business 1/	64	65	77	69	65	**81**	75	N	75%
Percentage of importers identified by TTB as illegally operating without a federal permit	15%	15%	14%	13%	14%	**11%**	12%	Y	121%

DISC - Discontinued

1/ FY 2011 and FY 2012 Actuals have been revised based on an error in the source data. The revised actual for FY 2011 is 77 days (not 74) and the revised actual for FY 2012 is 69 days (not 67).

Performance Discussion

In FY 2013, TTB met two of its three annual targets for the performance measures under the Protect the Public budget activity. TTB tracks its success in meeting its trade advancement and consumer protection goals through three principal performance measures that indicate how timely the Bureau is in issuing permits to qualified alcohol and tobacco businesses, how effective TTB is in deterring illicit importation of tobacco products by non-permitted entities, and the efficiency of the Bureau's alcohol beverage label application processing activity. Taken together, these measures reflect the priorities of a service-oriented organization that applies technology to the greatest extent to perform its consumer protection role and to ensure that commerce is fair, lawful, and open. TTB's strategies to achieve its performance targets in this budget activity include a combination of streamlining its internal procedures, implementing enhancements to its online filing systems, and publishing clear guidance to industry members.

Improve Efficiency and Effectiveness of Permitting Process

TTB protects consumers by screening permit applicants to ensure only qualified persons engage in operations in the alcohol and tobacco industries. For this purpose, in FY 2013, TTB processed approximately 7,700 original and 18,000 amended permits, and performed 275 investigations into high-risk applicants to meet TTB's business integrity objective. TTB monitors its timeliness in processing permit applications through its measure of the Average Number of Days to Process an Original Permit Application for a New Alcohol or Tobacco Business. Undue delays in permit application processing impede economic growth, primarily in the small business sector, as taxable commodities such as finished wine, beer, or spirits products cannot be lawfully produced without a federal permit from TTB. TTB targeted a 65-day turnaround time for original permit applications in FY 2013, but resource challenges resulted in average processing times of 81 days.

TTB completed its rollout of the Permits Online system in FY 2012, with the dual goals of improving permit processing times and increasing the number of paperless transactions with the business community

TTB serves. Over the past several years, however, the volume of applications has increased, making it difficult to maintain service levels, particularly given recent budget constraints. Between 2008 and 2011, TTB experienced an average annual increase of 3 percent in original permit applications. In FY 2012, however, the number of original permit applications received increased 33 percent, primarily due to growth in the craft brewer and alcohol wholesaler segments. In FY 2013, following a year of unprecedented growth, original permit applications remain well above the five-year average.

Even with greater than anticipated adoption rates for the Permits Online system, which reached 70 percent for the year, TTB does not anticipate achieving sustained reductions to its permit application turnaround time until various additional system enhancements are implemented in the latter quarters of FY 2015. Rather, the immediate benefit of Permits Online has been cost savings, with system efficiencies contributing to nearly $1 million in budget reductions. Although these reductions (equivalent to 9 full-time positions) have produced budget savings, they have slowed anticipated improvements in service delivery. TTB projects to average 75 days to process an original permit application at the close of FY 2014. Given the demand for TTB service, and the reductions to TTB staff, the targeted performance level will demonstrate TTB's effectiveness and the success of its new e-filing system, without which processing times would exceed 90 - 120 days.

Streamline Permit Qualification Process

TTB intends to meet the FY 2014 performance target through a combination of streamlining its internal procedures, engaging in industry outreach, and implementing ongoing system enhancements. TTB will also update its risk model and the procedures used to process permit applications, adding new financial data sources and improving the risk criteria used to vet applicants for suitability to hold a federal permit in the alcohol and tobacco industries. Increased focus on risk modeling and statistical sampling will help TTB maintain its assurance that it is permitting only qualified applicants while improving the efficiency of TTB's permit qualification process. In addition, TTB will continue to promote use of the Permits Online system by all permit applicants, including through webinars and online training.

Electronic Permit Filing

TTB also understands that the customer experience with Permits Online is a critical driver of adoption rates. TTB routinely updates the business rules and customer support features embedded in the system to help prospective industry members submit complete and accurate permit application information. By receiving complete applications, TTB can reduce the time spent returning applications to customers for correction and reviewing corrected submissions, thus improving the overall time from initial application submission to permit issuance.

TTB is also taking steps to speed its transition to an entirely online processing environment. System enhancements in development for fiscal years 2014 and 2015 include the data upload of historical permit application data from TTB's legacy permit and tax database to the Permits Online system. This initiative will allow the approximately 60,000 TTB permittees who originally filed a paper permit application to file for amendments to their permit (i.e., change in control or change in address) electronically through Permits Online. As TTB receives an average of 18,000 – 20,000 permit amendments annually, this project will result in efficiencies for both TTB and the businesses it serves.

Ensure Compliance with Importer Permit Requirement

Maintaining lawful operations in the trade of alcohol and tobacco commodities is a principal TTB objective. TTB continues its enforcement of federal permit requirements, targeting entities identified as importing cigarettes and other tobacco products without a TTB permit. Through its measure of Percentage of Importers Identified by TTB as Illegally Operating without a Federal Permit, TTB monitors CBP's International Trade Data System and compares the import data to the permittees on file with TTB, which enables the Bureau to identify and take action against entities engaging in unlawful operations. In FY 2013, TTB set a performance target of 14 percent for this measure. TTB met its target, as just 11 percent of entities reporting importations of tobacco products had done so without a permit. The vast majority of unpermitted importers consist of individuals purchasing tobacco products from overseas via the Internet. TTB's issuance of cease and desist letters, and appropriate follow up activities, ensured that the responsible parties ended operations or obtained a permit.

TTB intends to meet its FY 2014 performance target of 12 percent for this measure by continuing to monitor and take action to address imports of tobacco products by non-permitted parties. These efforts support the enforcement of federal laws designed to prevent tobacco smuggling and to ensure the collection of all taxes levied on tobacco products. TTB also will continue to focus its enforcement efforts on the importation of processed tobacco to ensure that importers comply with federal law. Processed tobacco is the subject of intense TTB enforcement scrutiny, as it is a non-taxpaid tobacco product that may be diverted for illegal manufacturing purposes. Beginning in FY 2014, TTB will incorporate import data into its risk models for audit and investigation targets to help deter illegal importations of tobacco.

Improve Efficiency and Effectiveness of Alcohol Beverage Label Processing

TTB protects U.S. consumers by ensuring that alcohol beverage products offered at retail outlets are properly labeled and comply with federal production standards. This activity also facilitates compliant trade, as a TTB label approval is required before an industry member can introduce their products into interstate commerce. In FY 2013, TTB met both objectives through the approval of 118,800 of the 140,300 COLA applications received; the remaining applications were rejected, returned for correction, withdrawn, or expired. In furtherance of the Treasury-wide goal to increase paperless transactions, the Bureau targeted and met its performance level of 92 percent electronic filing for COLA applications. The ongoing rise in electronic filing is due to system improvements made in response to customer feedback that simplify the filing process for industry members.

TTB has set an FY 2014 performance target of 93 percent for this measure and, to meet this performance goal, the Bureau will use targeted outreach to reach the segments of the industry that have not migrated to the online filing environment. In FY 2013, TTB modified its internal operating procedures to process paper label applications electronically. This move to a paperless processing environment has improved communications with industry members regarding rejected applications or applications that TTB returns to the applicant for correction.

Even with high rates of electronic filing, the volume of label applications necessitates consideration of broader efforts to streamline the alcohol beverage label application process. Between 2008 and 2012, the number of applications increased by 14 percent. Actions taken in FY 2013 to expand the number and type of changes that industry may make to an alcohol beverage label without submitting a new COLA application reduced the volume of submissions by 8 percent compared to the prior year. Though TTB labeling program changes in 2012 and 2013 were successful in bending the curve for label applications, rapid annual growth in the industry may cause label applications to increase in the future. Addressing the volume of label applications requires TTB to continue its efforts to update and streamline its labeling program. Through other changes to its forms, guidance, and internal processing procedures, as well as a planned modernization of the federal alcohol labeling regulations, the Bureau will prepare to shift from a pre-approval process for reviewing label applications to a more useful marketplace review of labels. By redirecting resources to marketplace enforcement, TTB intends to improve program results by continuing to ensure that labels that reach consumers are accurate and not deceptive while improving service by reducing the time it takes industry to enter compliantly labeled alcohol beverages into the marketplace. TTB plans to publish a proposed modernization of its labeling and advertising regulations in FY 2015.

Summary of Management and Organizational Excellence Performance

Effectively and efficiently administering the Bureau's revenue collection and public protection mission requires that TTB create the conditions necessary for programs to reach and sustain excellence. In all aspects of performing its mission, TTB aims to ensure that its programs operate efficiently and effectively, and with full accountability. TTB accomplishes this by providing program offices with the high-quality management and administrative support needed to achieve the Bureau's program goals.

The Bureau's objectives in the area of Management and Organizational Excellence align with the Administration's emphasis on automating processes to improve services and enhancing internal operations to be more efficient and effective. In FY 2013, TTB demonstrated its ability to enhance efficiency and reduce costs through its strategic management of human capital, IT enhancements to improve operations, and rigorous financial management practices.

Human Capital Management

TTB continues to implement the strategic goals, strategies, and measures outlined in the current Human Capital Strategic Plan. As the majority of TTB's human resource functions are operated through the Bureau of the Fiscal Service Administrative Resource Center (ARC), TTB establishes and updates, as appropriate, performance benchmarks and measures to monitor these outsourced functions. In FY 2014, TTB will complete its 2014-2017 Human Capital Strategic Plan to align with the strategic direction of the Bureau. The new plan takes into account the overall business and cultural vision for TTB, to include:

- Addressing retirement trends by identifying and closing competency gaps and creating a succession plan, enhancing our recruitment and retention plan, and identifying targeted skills sets;

- Providing an employee-friendly culture that strikes an appropriate work/life balance through employee recognition, performance management, flexible schedules, and teleworking;

- Incorporating organizational needs into human capital planning as identified by the OPM Employee Viewpoint Survey results; and

- Streamlining human resource functions through various information systems, including a new electronic employee official personnel file, performance management system, and enhanced online availability of self-service personnel actions.

Employee satisfaction is critical to a productive workplace. Each year, the Office of Personnel Management (OPM) administers the Federal Employee Viewpoint Survey (FEVS) to measure the satisfaction of the federal workforce. The TTB FEVS average score for FY 2013 trended down to a 74.7 percent positive response rate from employees, a decrease from 77.1 percent in FY 2012. TTB will develop an FY 2013 FEVS Action Plan to address areas in the survey that showed a decline from the prior year.

Based on this survey data, the Partnership for Public Service determines rankings for federal agencies. TTB ranked 25th out of 300 sub-component agencies on the FY 2013 Best Places to Work in the Federal Government rankings, a decrease from its 2012 ranking of 15 out of 292.

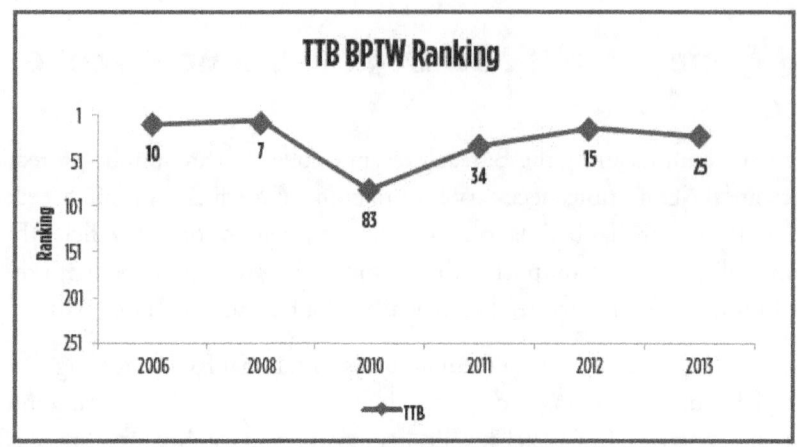

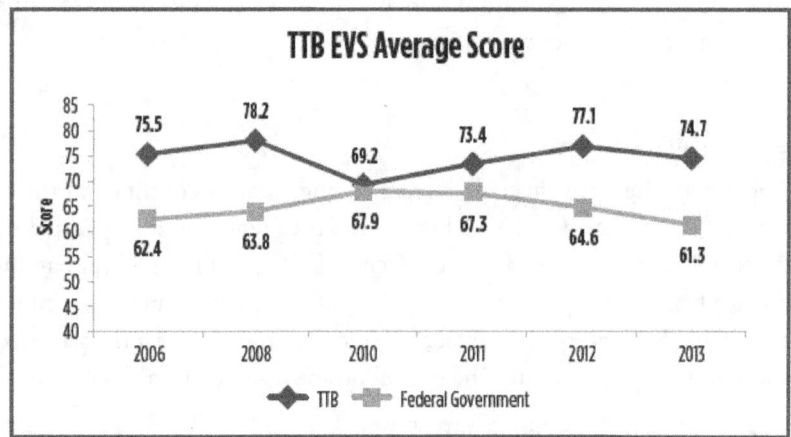

The reported scores indicate the average of three survey items
that identify overall employee satisfaction.

In its efforts to improve employee satisfaction, TTB used survey results to identify key actions for its FY 2013 FEVS Action Plan. TTB targeted the areas of internal communications and workforce engagement to sustain the improvements in employee satisfaction realized in these areas in FY 2012. During FY 2013, TTB:

- Continued its development and implementation of its new strategic plan, developed using a collaborative process that involves the participation of a Core Team of employees from across the Bureau and the TTB executive team;

- Implemented a comprehensive communications strategy to promote understanding of TTB's strategic objectives and priorities, which included NTEU briefings, a TTB-wide virtual town hall meeting, and several Strategy Forums with the workforce;

- Launched an online resource center and reported progress on the strategy, performance results, and planned priority initiatives through online postings. The resource center provides updates on performance measures through an online dashboard that is accessible by all employees; and

- Initiated the development of a formal communications program, with strategies for both internal and external stakeholders, to sustain improvements in survey scores made over the past two years.

Implementing these and other initiatives in the FY 2013 FEVS Action Plan increased communication to employees, ensured a highly talented and well-developed staff, and enhanced employee engagement.

As a knowledge-intensive organization, TTB requires a highly trained workforce to fulfill its responsibility to protect the public and collect the revenue within a dynamic and global environment. During FY 2013, TTB used a variety of human capital policies and programs for recruiting and attracting talent to ensure qualified people with the necessary skills are in the right positions, and to continue to retain those professionals in the future. Successful strategies included partnerships with a diverse range of universities across the country and use of the Treasury Veterans Program.

Succession planning is also a strategic priority for the Bureau, especially as it relates to TTB's mission-critical positions. One in three TTB employees is eligible to retire in FY 2014. TTB continued its Emerging Leaders Program (ELP), established in FY 2009. This leadership development initiative offers three unique certificate programs for non-supervisors, first-level supervisors, and second-level managers at TTB. The three-year program series supports TTB's succession planning strategies and prepares participants with the competencies critical for higher levels of leadership responsibility. Based on participant feedback, TTB is working on expanding the program's offerings to include mentoring opportunities and detail assignments to broaden the exposure of program participants.

The FY 2014 President's Budget proposed the discontinuance of the pilot pay-for-performance program at TTB, a program originally authorized in 1999 and that had been in operation at TTB since the Bureau was established in 2003. Since this program did not originate as an OPM pilot pay-for-performance system, and as such had not been subject to direct OPM oversight, the Administration did not support the continuation of the program. The Administration suggested that TTB petition OPM for authorization to pilot a new demonstration project and to use the results of a five-year pilot program to determine whether a permanent program should be established at TTB. In FY 2013, as required by law, TTB negotiated with the National Treasury Employees Union (NTEU) to terminate the existing pay demonstration project. As TTB believes pay-for-performance aligns with its results-driven culture, TTB will work jointly with the Department of the Treasury and OPM to develop a sound business strategy to implement a permanent pay-for-performance program at the Bureau.

Financial Management

TTB established and monitored key performance standards to ensure that its business activities covering financial accounting and reporting operate in a highly effective and efficient manner. In FY 2013, TTB achieved all of its financial management performance metrics, in collaboration with its shared service provider, the Bureau of the Fiscal Service Administrative Resource Center.

This joint effort in providing financial management services has allowed TTB to meet its financial goals and deliver quality accounting and budget services to program staff, including:

- Paying vendor invoices on time (Prompt Payment Rate) greater than 99 percent;

- Achieving an Electronic Fund Transfer Compliance Rate of greater than 99 percent;

- Ensuring a Proper Payments Rate of greater than 99 percent;

- Processing Budget Reprogramming Documents within 2 business days;

- Completing timely entry of budget and financial data in the OMB MAX reporting system;

- Reconciling Cash Account by the 4th calendar day of the month;

- Ensuring prompt deposits and recording of tax collections; and

- Providing timely and useful financial management data.

TTB also met established due dates to ensure timely submission of reports required by the Bureau of the Fiscal Service. Monthly closing of financial data was completed within three business days, and payroll information was downloaded into the core accounting system within three working days of receipt from the National Finance Center.

Joint reviews of payroll activity were conducted to obtain reliable projections of payroll costs relative to continuously changing on-board staffing levels. The payroll projection system has proven to be a valuable tool, and its use has led to better financial information for budget decision making and helped the Bureau avoid Anti-Deficiency Act violations. The ability to extract information from the core accounting system and make sound payroll projections continues to provide reliable and accurate financial information for TTB management to use in executing the budget.

In FY 2013, TTB was also able to conduct timely reviews of financial information so that program offices were provided with the data necessary to make efficient use of the bureau's annual appropriation and fulfill TTB's tax collection and regulatory responsibilities, as outlined in its budget plan. By closely monitoring the Bureau's financial status, TTB was successful in making a number of key investments to support its mission. These financial reviews were not limited to the current year's appropriation. TTB also conducted a review of prior year obligations because up to 50 percent of unobligated funds from a prior year may be accessed for critical and/or unforeseen investments with appropriate authorization. In FY 2013, TTB received authorization for $790 thousand from unobligated FY 2012 funds to invest in its Permits Online system and in IT hardware equipment.

In support of Treasury's OMB Circular A-123 requirements over financial reporting controls, the TTB Office of Finance and Performance Budgeting tested internal controls related to the financial reporting of tax collections. The review identified no control weaknesses over TTB's collection activity and the reporting of those collections.

Expansion of Technology Solutions

TTB made significant progress in achieving its strategic vision of using technology to streamline the delivery of its critical lines of business and to support data-driven decision making. In FY 2013, TTB continued with business application development to support improvements to the permit, formula, and label application processes in order to reduce the regulatory burden on industry members.

In FY 2013, TTB completed two major releases of the Permits Online system. Among other things, these system updates enabled industry members to download an encrypted electronic copy of their application data. After receiving their federal permit, industry members may then submit their permit data to state liquor authorities in applying for equivalent state licenses. For example, applicants intending to operate in the state of Kentucky may now upload their federal application data into their state application, reducing the burden of data entry. TTB also added functionality to assist customers in identifying and filing required supplemental documents with each electronic application. Depending on the commodity, these documents may include items such as corporate documents, bank statements, trade name registrations, and premise descriptions. TTB also made it easier for customers to view and copy information, which assists industry members with multiple permits or locations.

Going forward, TTB will continue to improve the usage rate of Permits Online through outreach efforts and system enhancements that improve the system's functionality for both external and internal users. Significantly, TTB is in the process of developing and testing enhancements that will enable approximately 60,000 active industry members to use Permits Online to electronically file an amendment to their permit. Given that TTB receives approximately 18,000 permit amendments annually, TTB anticipates that this system enhancement will result in efficiencies for both TTB and industry members.

TTB also works to continuously improve COLAs Online, recognizing the importance of issuing timely approvals for alcohol beverage labels that comply with federal requirements. Also, over time, improving and streamlining the processing of electronic applications will facilitate TTB's planned transition to a market-based review of labels for both TTB and the regulated industries. In FY 2013, TTB added system validations to ensure compliant COLA applications, enhanced search options to assist industry with obtaining access to their COLAs, and improved the view of pending applications by adding new sorting capabilities.

TTB has also integrated features of COLAs Online with its electronic system for filing formula applications, Formulas Online. Many alcohol beverages require formula approval prior to the issuance of a COLA and, to simplify this process, Formulas Online allows industry members to link their approved formulas to COLAs Online when they file for label approval. In FY 2013, TTB made multiple improvements to Formulas Online, including enhancements to user registration; an upgrade to the search function; and changes to the print, work list, submission summary, and user notification features. TTB will continue to review and enhance Formulas Online to provide an even more efficient and user-friendly electronic filing venue for industry members. Through its planned industry forums, TTB intends to develop both short- and long-term initiatives to make the Formulas Online system more functional for external and internal users.

As part of TTB's effort to maintain a state of the art laboratory environment, TTB initiated a project in FY 2011 to replace the existing Laboratory Information Management System (LIMS), a platform for consolidating sample analysis data for the four laboratories that comprise the Bureau's Scientific Services Division. The new system integrates with laboratory instruments and provides a secure process that facilitates the electronic collection and processing of sample analyses. The LIMS 2.0 system is also crucial to maintaining the laboratory's international accreditation status, as it streamlines the process, review, and disposition of sample analyses to ensure compliance with ISO 17025 accreditation. Other benefits include chemical inventory management for the disposal or destruction of reagents and chemicals and robust reporting capabilities to support the effective management of laboratory process workflows.

In support of the Department of the Treasury's technology modernization campaign, TTB worked toward improving program results and reducing overall operating costs in FY 2013 through its ongoing support of "cloud computing" initiatives. Cloud computing is a model for enabling convenient, on-demand network access to a shared pool of configurable computing resources (e.g., networks, servers, storage, applications, and services) that can be rapidly provisioned and released with minimal management effort or service provider interaction. The Bureau is developing TTB's private cloud by building its virtualized infrastructure and cloud software service as well as a community cloud by hosting and providing cloud infrastructure as a service to the Community Development Financial Institutions (CDFI) Fund.

TTB's network infrastructure operates on a "virtual desktop" that centralizes all computing power, applications, user data, and user settings, which allows Bureau employees to access to TTB resources through thin client computing devices. A thin client is a computing device or program that relies on another device for computational power. Currently about 70 percent of TTB personnel use thin client devices to access all TTB applications and data. Certain TTB users, particularly investigators and auditors who operate in the field, are not candidates for the virtual desktop solution due to intermittent Web access. In FY 2013, TTB piloted a solution that may enable TTB to extend the benefits of the virtual desktop infrastructure to all TTB users, which will make the TTB network and hardware inventory more manageable, reliable, and secure.

As the IT service provider for CDFI, TTB made improvements in FY 2013 that increased CDFI's telework capabilities and improved its ability to collaborate with industry members and other bureaus, while achieving cost savings for the government. In February 2013, TTB implemented video teleconferencing capabilities and a Voice over Internet Protocol (VoIP) phone system to CDFI. As a result, CDFI users are no longer tied to their geographical locations; they can make calls from any location with access to the Internet and can conduct face-to-face meetings via the new video teleconferencing and VoIP infrastructure.

These cloud computing efforts have been critical to TTB's effective telework program, one of the most robust telework programs within the Department of the Treasury. TTB's workforce is widely dispersed, with many personnel working from home full time and over 80 percent of the workforce regularly teleworking. Advancements in TTB's IT network completed in FY 2013 have both improved the effectiveness of TTB's telework program and contributed to the Administration's goals under the "Bring Your Own Device" initiative of improving mobile work capabilities and reducing IT costs across government.

Message from the Chief Financial Officer

As the Nation continues to recover from a prolonged economic downturn, it is incumbent upon Government to lead the way in demonstrating responsible fiscal stewardship through sound management, efficient operations, and smarter and more streamlined services to its constituencies. To be more results oriented and performance driven, we continue to place more reliance on evidence based decision making and the use of such performance tools as dashboards. This has contributed to better choices that are rooted in facts and evidence. Though we have much to be proud of, as evidenced in this report, the Bureau continues to strive for continuous improvement through sound strategic planning, effective application of technology, and strong fiscal discipline.

The Bureau has developed a compliance dashboard to provide a consistent and efficient means of calculating and reporting performance metrics and key workload statistics for TTB managers and the clients that we serve. This transparency is an integral part of ensuring accountability and improvement of our client services.

Recognizing that we are responsible for producing results for every dollar entrusted to us, it is more important than ever for TTB to examine its operations to ensure that we are efficiently managing our resources and returning value for the investments made in our mission. Assurance that we are effectively allocating limited resources to deliver on our mission requires a comprehensive organizational strategy to guide strategic decisions about our operations and policies. We have chosen to apply the Balanced Scorecard methodology to our planning process in order to integrate our strategic plan into our management and investment decisions to ensure TTB's long-term effectiveness. This tool provides a comprehensive management framework to assist in making decisions regarding where to direct our limited resources to achieve the greatest impact in moving the Bureau forward. By effectively using the data provided by the Balanced Scorecard and maintaining open dialogue about our strategy, we will be able to readily identify issues and opportunities and take targeted actions to improve the organization as a whole.

During Fiscal Year 2013, the Bureau operated under a continuing resolution until March 27, 2013, requiring us to plan for multiple funding scenarios, and to determine program implications surrounding those actions. The Bureau had to operate for most of the year, under a blanket of uncertainty, as to its level of resources for operations for the year, which was ultimately resolved when mid- way through the fiscal year, Congress enacted a Full Year Continued Resolution, which was combined with sequestration and rescission cuts. Extensive planning was necessary to absorb those budget reductions within a short time frame to ensure the Bureau would operate within its available financial resources and fulfill its mission.

To compound the circumstances, increasingly talks about a government shutdown over the debt ceiling and discretionary spending caps meant the Bureau had to invest a great deal of time to develop a plan that would provide for an orderly shutdown. Many believed a government shutdown would not occur when spending authority expired on September 30, but continual prudent planning was necessary in case it did happen. This plan provided instructions on how operations and personnel would be affected, and what services and functions of the Bureau would need to continue even in the absence of an enacted appropriation. In the absence of funding, the vast majority of the Bureau employees, not engaged in excepted activities under the Antideficiency Act, were furloughed. The excepted service provision could only be applied at the Bureau to tax collections, so the plan had to cover a shutdown and curtailment of most routine operations. These plan documents were subjected to a series of reviews both inside and outside of the Bureau.

In FY 2013, TTB again received an unmodified audit opinion on its financial statements from an independent public accounting firm, and they reported no significant deficiencies or material weaknesses in internal controls over financial reporting. Our support of this annual audit affirms our commitment to a vigorous internal control environment and financial reporting excellence. Further evidence of this commitment lies in our management practices, which include routine evaluations of our tax collection and revenue accounting operations at the National Revenue Center. These evaluations validate that sound internal and administrative controls are in place to ensure the collection and verification of $22.9 billion in annual Federal excise tax collections from alcohol, tobacco, firearms and ammunition industry members.

Even as resources contract, TTB will continue to aim high and put in place improved processes and tools to meet our mission. In the years ahead, strategic investments and sound planning will support the Bureau in improving the management and performance of this organization. Providing superior administrative support services while meeting our financial management improvement goals, while operating within our available resources is critical to producing sound agency performance results and providing taxpayer value. We remain optimistic about the continued opportunities to develop and implement new ideas for improving the management and performance of this Bureau and to more effectively integrate performance management across our programs.

Cheri D. Mitchell

Cheri D. Mitchell

Assistant Administrator, Management/CFO

Part III:
Financial Results, Position, Condition, and Auditors' Reports

Budget Highlights by Fund Account

FY 2013 Salaries and Expenses

Fund Source:	
Salaries & Expenses FY 2013	
Appropriation (P.L. 113-6, Consolidated and Further Continuing Appropriations Act, 2013) 1/	$99,878,000
Sequestration (P.L. 112-25, Budget Control Act of 2011)	$(5,024,463)
Across-the-Board Rescission (P.L. 113-6, Sec. 3004 (C)(1))	$(199,756)
Salaries & Expenses FY 2013 (Net)	**$94,653,781**
Obligations Incurred in FY 2013 from Current Year Appropriations	$93,809,000
Salaries & Expenses FY 2012/13 **(50% Prior Year Recovery) 2/**	**$790,000**
Obligations Incurred in FY 2013 from Current Year Appropriations	$790,000

1/ P.L. 113-6 included $2 million in funding for TTB to use for the costs of special law enforcement agents to target tobacco smuggling and other criminal diversion activities.

2/ General Provisions of the appropriations bill provide that 50 percent of the unobligated balances remaining available at the end of Fiscal Year 2012 shall remain available through September 30, 2013.

In FY 2013, TTB received $99,878,000 in direct appropriations under the Full-Year Continuing Appropriations Act, 2013, less the sequestration amount ($5,024,463) and less the rescission amount of ($199,756), which provided a total of $94,653,781. This amount included $1,895,388 for the costs of special law enforcement agents to target tobacco smuggling and other criminal diversion activities. TTB elected not to hire the agents directly, but to enter into an interagency agreement with the Internal Revenue Service Criminal Investigation office to conduct criminal investigations into violations of the tax laws TTB enforces. The authorized full-time equivalent (FTE) staffing level for direct positions was 482 in the FY 2013 President's Budget.

The budgeted amount maintains a program level consistent with the current level of effort necessary to support TTB's responsibility for revenue collection and the enforcement of laws and regulations governing alcohol and tobacco commodities.

The Bureau obligated or expended 99.1 percent of the $94,653,781 in FY 2013 direct funding from its one-year Salaries and Expenses appropriation.

Also during FY 2013, Congress authorized an additional $790,000 from the prior year account of unobligated available balances (often referred to as the 50 percent account) to cover a one-time investment in IT infrastructure to replace obsolete network equipment and enhancements to the Permits Online system.

Reimbursable Authority and Related Activities

During FY 2013, the Bureau realized reimbursable authority in the amount of $5.9 million. The primary sources of reimbursable funding were collections from the cover-over program and enforcement activity in Puerto Rico, investments in the TTB enforcement program from the Executive Office of Asset Forfeiture, and reimbursement from CDFI for information technology services.

Puerto Rico Cover-Over and Enforcement Activities

All costs associated with the functioning and support of the Puerto Rico office are paid from the cover-over program, which is offset from cover-over taxes collected in the United States on products originating in Puerto Rico ($349 million) and the Virgin Islands ($9 million).

In Puerto Rico, TTB conducts annual audits and investigations of industry members regarding the collection of revenue, application processing, and product integrity. Revenue inspections are used to conduct tax examinations on major producers of alcohol and tobacco. This is critical due to the requirements of verifying tax payments under the Internal Revenue Code (IRC), as well as TTB's subsequent accountability for all cover-over amounts due to the government of Puerto Rico.

All distilled spirits producers and processors, wineries, wholesalers, importers, Manufacturer of Nonbeverage Products claimants, and specially denatured alcohol permit applicants are subject to a qualification inspection under the IRC.

Additionally, major producers of distilled spirits, wine, and malt beverages are subject to inspection and audits in Puerto Rico.

Linking Budget and Program Spending

TTB has two primary budget activities: collecting all the Federal tax revenue due on alcohol, tobacco, firearms, and ammunition products and protecting consumers of alcohol beverages. Assisting industry members to understand and comply with the Federal laws and regulations regarding the commodities TTB regulates is an integral part of both activities.

In FY 2013, TTB used an account code structure that provides a direct link from the Bureau budget to specific programs and project activities. An analysis of the data stemming from the account code structure shows that, in FY 2013, TTB incurred obligations of $93,809,000 of its salaries and expenses appropriation, of which 53 percent was spent on the Collect the Revenue and 47 percent was spent on Protect the Public budget activities.

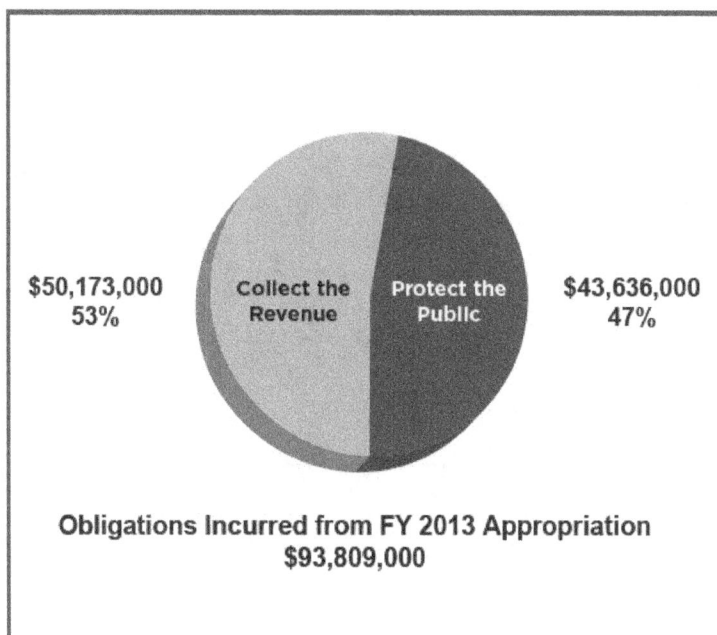

$50,173,000
53%

Collect the Revenue

Protect the Public

$43,636,000
47%

**Obligations Incurred from FY 2013 Appropriation
$93,809,000**

In order to ascertain the full costs of each of these budget activities, the overhead costs were allocated and combined with the direct program costs. TTB arrived at the overhead allocation by applying the pro rata share of the number of direct program dollars to each overhead cost category. The overhead is comprised of three major cost components: 1) general and administrative costs; 2) legal costs; and 3) information technology costs. The general and administrative category consists of costs related to operating the human resources, finance, procurement, training, facilities management, and other support-type functions.

Spending by Major Object Class

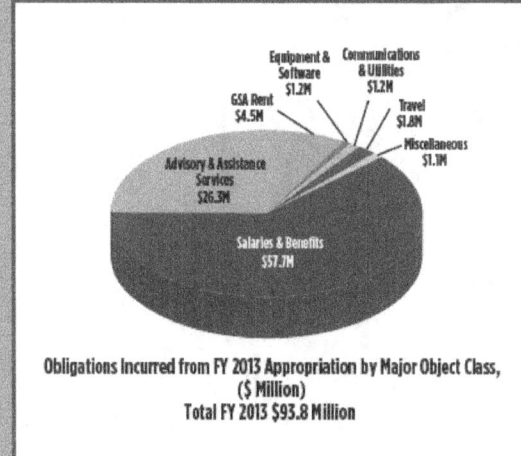

Equipment & Software $1.2M

Communications & Utilities $1.2M

GSA Rent $4.5M

Travel $1.8M

Advisory & Assistance Services $26.3M

Miscellaneous $1.1M

Salaries & Benefits $57.7M

**Obligations Incurred from FY 2013 Appropriation by Major Object Class,
($ Million)
Total FY 2013 $93.8 Million**

TTB presents its obligations incurred by budget activity and program in its Annual Report to explain the cost of delivering the services that support the mission. TTB also presents specific data regarding the purchase of goods and services by major object class that support its program activities. The majority of TTB's incurred obligations (90 percent) fall into two principal major object classes: Salaries & Benefits and Advisory & Assistance Services (Contracts). Salaries & Benefits comprise 62 percent of total obligations incurred by object class, and cover the cost of TTB's roughly 466 full-time equivalent positions in FY 2013. The Advisory & Assistance Services object class constitutes 28 percent of FY 2013 incurred obligations, and covers the cost of both commercial and intra-governmental services.

The commercial contracts category is predominantly IT contracts in support of engineering, infrastructure, and support services. This category includes other commercial contracts for services such as the scanning and imaging of label applications and tax forms, lab maintenance, and Web site development.

Intra-governmental services include administrative support services provided by our shared service provider for human resources, accounting, travel, and procurement. Other intra-governmental services include the costs for special agent support, background investigations, and Federal protective services. In FY 2013, the Bureau's travel costs were primarily related to its audits and investigations. The remaining object classes that cover the FY 2013 obligations incurred include those cost categories for rent, communications, equipment, and other miscellaneous categories.

Obligations Incurred from FY 2013 Appropriations by Budget Activity

Collect the Revenue..... $50,173,000

The Collect the Revenue budget activity encompasses TTB's revenue strategy and goal to provide the most effective and efficient system for the collection of all revenue that is rightfully due. It is also designed to prevent or eliminate tax evasion and other criminal conduct and provide high-quality service while imposing the least regulatory burden.

Under the Collect the Revenue activity, TTB administers three programs: 1) Alcohol and Tobacco Tax; 2) Firearms and Ammunitions Excise Tax (FAET); and 3) Outreach and Voluntary Compliance.

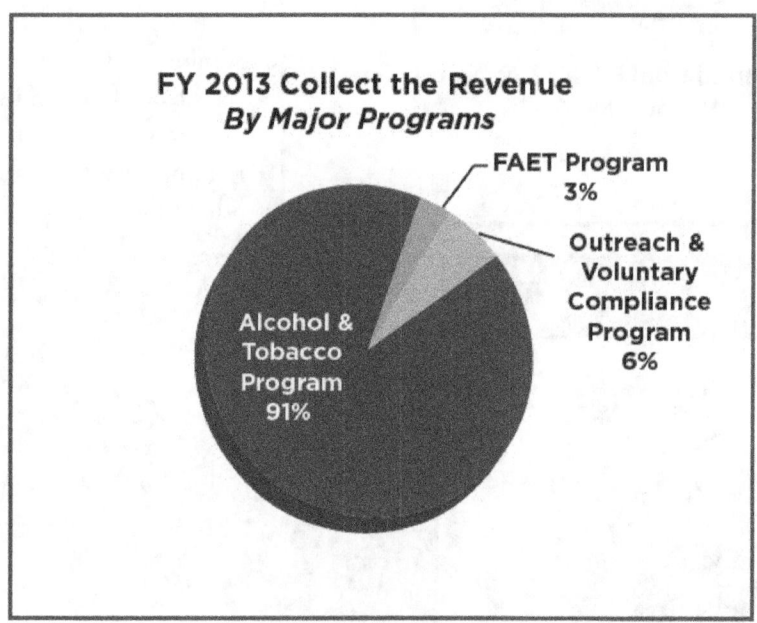

In FY 2013, TTB expended 91 percent of its Collect the Revenue resources in collecting Federal excise taxes from the alcohol and tobacco industries and 3 percent in collecting FAET. The specific projects that comprise these costs include the processing of tax returns and operational reports at the National Revenue Center and the audits and investigations conducted on industry.

Costs for the Outreach and Voluntary Compliance Program reached 6 percent of our Collect the Revenue resources. These resources went toward efforts to educate and train industry members regarding their obligations in the areas of tax calculations and remittance.

Protect the Public..... $43,636,000

The Protect the Public budget activity encompasses TTB's strategy and goal to ensure industry compliance with laws and regulations designed to protect the consumers of alcohol beverages.

TTB does this by assuring the integrity of the people who operate these businesses, of the products themselves, and of the marketplace in which they are traded.

TTB administers four programs under the Protect the Public budget activity: 1) Permits and Business Assurance; 2) Advertising, Labeling, and Product Safety; 3) Trade Facilitation; and 4) Outreach and Voluntary Compliance.

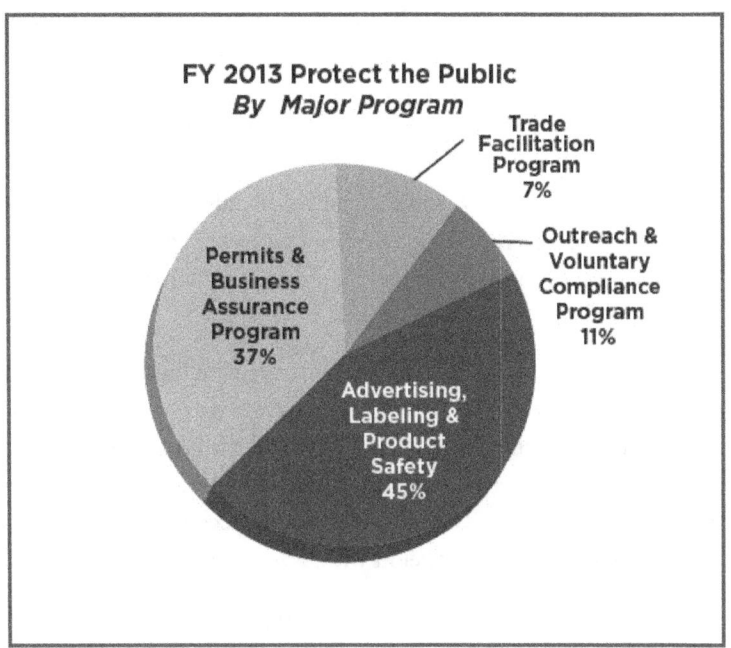

An analysis of the financial data from FY 2013 reveals that TTB spent the preponderance of its Protect the Public resources on two programs: Labeling, Advertising, and Product Safety at 45 percent, and Permits and Business Assurance at 37 percent.

The Labeling, Advertising, and Product Safety Program includes activities designed to assure that beverage alcohol labels fully and accurately describe the products upon which they appear and are not misleading. It also encompasses activities to verify that alcohol advertisements contain all mandatory information and do not mislead consumers. The Product Safety component involves all investigative and laboratory activities performed as part of the Alcohol Beverage Safety and Verification Program, including work related to domestic and imported product analysis.

The Permits and Business Assurance Program is designed to determine the eligibility of persons wishing to enter any of the businesses TTB regulates and to process applications for changes to the original permit. These activities may include a field investigation. The permit is necessary in order to conduct operations in the regulated industries.

The remainder of the Protect the Public resources were divided between the Trade Facilitation Program (7 percent) and the Outreach and Voluntary Compliance Program (11 percent).

Systems and Controls

Introduction

During FY 2013, TTB contracted with the Bureau of the Fiscal Service (BFS) Administrative Resource Center (ARC) to handle its administrative, human resources, procurement, travel and, financial functions.

Accounting Systems and Controls

The BFS ARC accounting system, known as Oracle Federal Financials, is certified by the Financial Systems Integration Office (FSIO) requirements and is in full compliance with Treasury reporting requirements; it also meets requirements under the Federal Financial Management Improvement Act (FFMIA).

The FY 2013 audit of Treasury's consolidated financial statements, which covered the financial management systems of our service provider, BFS ARC, did not identify any instances in which ARC's financial management systems did not substantially comply with FFMIA. Specifically, no instances were identified in which ARC's financial management systems did not substantially comply with 1) Federal financial management systems requirements, 2) applicable Federal accounting standards, and 3) the United States Government Standard General Ledger at the transaction level.

The Bureau successfully met the Department of the Treasury's reporting requirements and has maintained accurate and reliable financial information on TTB's program activities. The various administrative modules integrated with the TTB financial system have proven to accurately capture Bureau financial data and provide reliable information to management to inform decision making. Only two TTB databases operate outside the BFS ARC environment—the TTB property management system and the tax administration database, IRIS.

Federal Managers' Financial Integrity Act of 1982 (FMFIA)

The FMFIA requires Federal agencies to conduct ongoing evaluations of the systems of internal accounting and administrative control. Annually, TTB must report to Treasury all material weaknesses found through these evaluations. Treasury submits a consolidated report on the Department's controls to the President.

The FMFIA also requires the heads of agencies to provide the President with yearly assurance that obligations and costs are in compliance with applicable laws; that funds, property, and other assets are safeguarded against waste, loss, unauthorized use, or misappropriation; and revenues and expenditures are properly recorded and accounted for.

To provide this report and assurance to the President, the Secretary of the Treasury depends upon information from component heads regarding their management controls. The FMFIA program places reliance on each office at TTB to maintain a cost-effective system of controls to provide reasonable assurance that Government resources are protected against fraud, waste, abuse, mismanagement, or misappropriation.

Responsibilities of the Bureau's executive staff include ensuring that programs and administrative support activities are managed efficiently and effectively. Managers must conform to specific management accountability and improvement policies when designing, planning, organizing, and carrying out their responsibilities in order to ensure the most efficient and effective operation of their programs.

These policies address:

- Delegation of authority and responsibility;

- Hierarchical reporting of emerging management problems;

- Personal integrity;

- Quality data;

- Separation of key duties and responsibilities;

- Periodic comparisons of actual with recorded accountability of resources;

- Routine assessment of programs with a high potential for risk;

- Systematic review strategy to assess the effectiveness of program operations; and

- Prompt management actions to correct significant problems or improve operations.

Since its inception, TTB has gradually developed its own Bureau-specific policies.

Management accountability systems must assure basic compliance with the objectives of the FMFIA and the management control standards set by the Government Accountability Office. In addition, any inspection, audit, evaluation, peer or program review process, self-assessment, or the equivalent, used by TTB management to keep informed about needs and opportunities for improvement must incorporate these same standards into its methodology.

Furthermore, the Bureau completed an annual risk assessment for improper payments on all of its programs and activities. This process disclosed low risk susceptibility for improper payments, and documented that sound internal management and controls were in place at the Bureau to cover its disbursements.

The Bureau continues to strengthen and improve the execution of its mission through the application of sound internal controls over financial reporting. In response to OMB Circular A-123, Management's Responsibility for Internal Controls, the Bureau, in concert with the Department, developed and implemented an extensive testing and assessment methodology that identified and documented internal controls over financial reporting on our revenue accounting activities.

This increased emphasis on management controls has had a positive impact on programs and enabled the Bureau to achieve the intended results. The process also ensures that the utilization of resources is consistent with mission priorities and that program and resources are being used without waste, fraud, or mismanagement. Also, in addition to the A-123 review, TTB conducted a series of office reviews during FY 2013 that included an extensive review of administrative and internal controls.

Financial Statement Highlights

The following overview of the TTB financial statements highlights certain aspects of the financial statements for the fiscal year ended September 30, 2013.

- The Balance Sheet shows the assets, liabilities, and net position as of a point in time, in this case, as of September 30, 2013.

  - The total assets were reported as $72.0 million at the close of the fiscal year. Of this amount, $32.1 million is classified as the fund balance with Treasury. That fund balance account is the undisbursed account balance with the Treasury, primarily resulting from undisbursed appropriations.

  - The total liabilities amount reported is $41.8 million, of which total intragovernmental liabilities amounts to $17.9 million. The other liabilities are classified by type, such as accrued tax refunds, payables, and other liabilities.

  - The Statement of Net Cost shows the total net cost of operations at $100.9 million for the Bureau to administer its two budget activities.

    - The total net cost reported as program costs under the Collect the Revenue program was $48.2 million.

    - The total net cost reported as program costs under the Protect the Public program was $52.7 million.

  - The Statement of Change in Net Position shows a total net position balance of $30.1 million, and that amount represents the unexpended appropriations from both prior periods and from the current operating cycle in addition to Net Position from Operations.

  - The Statement of Budgetary Resources shows the budgetary resources received and the status of those resources. For TTB, the resources are primarily annual appropriations received from the in the amount of $94.7 million, in addition to spending authority from collections. The offsetting collections amount was $7.1 million. Of that amount, $3.2 million is from the recovery of costs for maintaining enforcement operations in Puerto Rico.

  - The Statement of Custodial Activity shows the amount of revenue received during FY 2013 compared with FY 2012, along with tax refunds, drawback on Manufacturer of Nonbeverage Products claims, and cover-over payments. The amount displayed shows that the total Federal excise tax revenues collected from alcohol, tobacco, firearms, and ammunition amounted to $22.9 billion. Within this total, the Bureau processed tax refunds, drawback claims, and cover-over payments in the amount of $738.7 million.

    - **Drawback claims** of $345.2 million were processed based on claims filed from MNBPs. Under current law, a drawback claim is allowed when distilled spirits on which the tax has been paid were unfit for beverage purposes and used in the production of medicines, medicinal preparations, food products, flavors, flavoring extracts, or perfumes.

    - **Tax refunds** and other adjustments (e.g., interest) were processed in the amount of $35.3 million.

- **Cover-over payments** were returned to Puerto Rico and the Virgin Islands in the amount of $357.7 million. Such taxes collected on rum imported in the United States are "covered over," or paid into, the treasuries of Puerto Rico and the Virgin Islands.

- **The disposition of the custodial revenue,** after refunds, claims, and cover-over payments, nets to $22.2 billion, and that amount was deposited to the U.S. Treasury to fund the Federal Government, with the exception of the Federal firearms and ammunition Federal excise taxes. Those revenues, in the amount of $762.7 million, were remitted to the Fish and Wildlife Restoration Fund under provisions of the Pittman Robertson Act of 1937.

Notes to the Basic Financial Statements

The notes to the basic financial statements provide additional information that is essential to a full understanding of the financial information provided in the statements.

Required Supplementary Information

In addition to the basic financial statements and accompanying notes, this report presents required supplementary information. For instance, TTB includes a table that outlines the tax collections for the past 10 years for each of the key revenue sources. Also, a table has been included to show the refunds, cover-over payments, and drawback payments for the past 10 years.

Financial Statements, Accompanying Notes, and Supplemental Information

Limitations of Financial Statements

The principal statements have been prepared to report the financial position and results of operations of the entity, pursuant to the requirements of 31 U.S.C. 3515(b). While the statements have been prepared from the books and records of the entity in accordance with GAAP for federal entities and the formats prescribed by the Office of Management and Budget (OMB), the statements are in addition to the financial reports used to monitor and control budgetary resources, which are prepared from the same books and records. For fiscal years 2013 and 2012, all financial statements and notes have been audited.

Management Responsibilities

Bureau management is responsible for the fair presentation of information contained in the principal financial statements, in conformity with generally accepted accounting principles (GAAP), and the form and content for entity financial statements specified by OMB in Circular A-136.

Management is also responsible for the fair representation of TTB's performance measures in accordance with OMB requirements. The quality of the Bureau's internal control structure rests with management, as does the responsibility for identification of and compliance with pertinent laws and regulations.

TTB in Relation to Treasury's Annual Financial Statements

The Department of the Treasury received an unmodified audit opinion on its FY 2013 financial statements. The financial activities of the Bureau are an integral part of the information reported by the Department of the Treasury.

This unmodified audit opinion means that the financial information presented by the Treasury, which includes TTB's financial activities, was presented fairly and in conformity with generally accepted accounting principles (GAAP) of the United States.

KPMG LLP
Suite 12000
1801 K Street, NW
Washington, DC 20006

Independent Auditors' Report

Inspector General
United States Department of the Treasury

Administrator
Alcohol and Tobacco Tax and Trade Bureau:

Report on the Financial Statements

We have audited the accompanying financial statements of the Alcohol and Tobacco Tax and Trade Bureau, which comprise the balance sheets as of September 30, 2013 and 2012, and the related statements of net cost, changes in net position, budgetary resources, and custodial activity, for the years then ended, and the related notes to the financial statements.

Management's Responsibility for the Financial Statements

Management is responsible for the preparation and fair presentation of these financial statements in accordance with U.S. generally accepted accounting principles; this includes the design, implementation, and maintenance of internal control relevant to the preparation and fair presentation of financial statements that are free from material misstatement, whether due to fraud or error.

Auditors' Responsibility

Our responsibility is to express an opinion on these financial statements based on our audits. We conducted our audits in accordance with auditing standards generally accepted in the United States of America; the standards applicable to financial audits contained in *Government Auditing Standards* issued by the Comptroller General of the United States; and Office of Management and Budget (OMB) Bulletin No. 14-02, *Audit Requirements for Federal Financial Statements*. Those standards and OMB Bulletin No. 14-02 require that we plan and perform the audit to obtain reasonable assurance about whether the financial statements are free from material misstatement.

An audit involves performing procedures to obtain audit evidence about the amounts and disclosures in the financial statements. The procedures selected depend on the auditors' judgment, including the assessment of the risks of material misstatement of the financial statements, whether due to fraud or error. In making those risk assessments, the auditor considers internal control relevant to the entity's preparation and fair presentation of the financial statements in order to design audit procedures that are appropriate in the circumstances, but not for the purpose of expressing an opinion on the effectiveness of the entity's internal control. Accordingly, we express no such opinion. An audit also includes evaluating the appropriateness of accounting policies used and the reasonableness of significant accounting estimates made by management, as well as evaluating the overall presentation of the financial statements.

We believe that the audit evidence we have obtained is sufficient and appropriate to provide a basis for our audit opinion.

Opinion on the Financial Statements

In our opinion, the financial statements referred to above present fairly, in all material respects, the financial position of the Alcohol and Tobacco Tax and Trade Bureau as of September 30, 2013 and 2012, and its net costs, changes in net position, budgetary resources, and custodial activity for the years then ended in accordance with U.S. generally accepted accounting principles.

Other Matters

Required Supplementary Information

U.S. generally accepted accounting principles require that the information in the Management's Discussion and Analysis, and Required Supplementary Information be presented to supplement the basic financial statements. Such information, although not a part of the basic financial statements, is required by the Federal Accounting Standards Advisory Board who considers it to be an essential part of financial reporting for placing the basic financial statements in an appropriate operational, economic, or historical context. We have applied certain limited procedures to the required supplementary information in accordance with auditing standards generally accepted in the United States of America, which consisted of inquiries of management about the methods of preparing the information and comparing the information for consistency with management's responses to our inquiries, the basic financial statements, and other knowledge we obtained during our audits of the basic financial statements. We do not express an opinion or provide any assurance on the information because the limited procedures do not provide us with sufficient evidence to express an opinion or provide any assurance.

Other Information

Our audits were conducted for the purpose of forming an opinion on the basic financial statements as a whole. The Other Accompanying Information included in (1) pages i through vii, (2) *Part II: Program Performance Results,* (3) *Message from the Chief Financial Officer,* (4) pages 65 through 74 and pages 108 through 112 of *Part III, Financial Results, Position, Condition and Auditors' Reports,* and (5) *Part IV: Appendices* is presented for purposes of additional analysis and is not a required part of the basic financial statements. Such information has not been subjected to the auditing procedures applied in the audit of the basic financial statements, and accordingly, we do not express an opinion or provide any assurance on it.

Other Reporting Required by *Government Auditing Standards*

In accordance with *Government Auditing Standards,* we have also issued our report dated January 30, 2014 on our consideration of the Alcohol and Tobacco Tax and Trade Bureau's internal control over financial reporting and our report dated January 30, 2014 on our tests of its compliance with certain provisions of laws, regulations, contracts, and other matters. The purpose of those reports is to describe the scope of our testing of internal control over financial reporting and compliance and the results of that testing, and not to provide an opinion on the internal control over financial reporting or on compliance. Those reports are an integral part of an audit performed in accordance with *Government Auditing Standards* in considering Alcohol and Tobacco Tax and Trade Bureau's internal control over financial reporting and compliance.

January 30, 2014

KPMG LLP
Suite 12000
1801 K Street, NW
Washington, DC 20006

Independent Auditors' Report on Internal Control Over Financial Reporting

Inspector General
United States Department of the Treasury

Administrator
Alcohol and Tobacco Tax and Trade Bureau:

We have audited, in accordance with auditing standards generally accepted in the United States of America; the standards applicable to financial audits contained in *Government Auditing Standards* issued by the Comptroller General of the United States; and Office of Management and Budget (OMB) Bulletin No. 14-02, *Audit Requirements for Federal Financial Statements*, the financial statements of Alcohol and Tobacco Tax and Trade Bureau, which comprise the balance sheets as of September 30, 2013 and 2012, and the related statements of net cost, changes in net position, budgetary resources, and custodial activity, for the years then ended, and the related notes to the financial statements, and have issued our report thereon dated January 30, 2014.

Internal Control Over Financial Reporting

In planning and performing our audit of the financial statements as of and for the year ended September 30, 2013, we considered the Alcohol and Tobacco Tax and Trade Bureau's internal control over financial reporting (internal control) to determine the audit procedures that are appropriate in the circumstances for the purpose of expressing our opinion on the financial statements, but not for the purpose of expressing an opinion on the effectiveness of the Alcohol and Tobacco Tax and Trade Bureau's internal control. Accordingly, we do not express an opinion on the effectiveness of the Alcohol and Tobacco Tax and Trade Bureau's internal control. We did not test all internal controls relevant to operating objectives as broadly defined by the *Federal Managers' Financial Integrity Act of 1982*.

A deficiency in internal control exists when the design or operation of a control does not allow management or employees, in the normal course of performing their assigned functions, to prevent, or detect and correct, misstatements on a timely basis. A material weakness is a deficiency, or a combination of deficiencies, in internal control, such that there is a reasonable possibility that a material misstatement of the entity's financial statements will not be prevented, or detected and corrected on a timely basis. A significant deficiency is a deficiency, or a combination of deficiencies, in internal control that is less severe than a material weakness, yet important enough to merit attention by those charged with governance.

Our consideration of internal control was for the limited purpose described in the first paragraph of this section and was not designed to identify all deficiencies in internal control that might be material weaknesses or significant deficiencies. Given these limitations, during our audit we did not identify any deficiencies in internal control that we consider to be material weaknesses. However, material weaknesses may exist that have not been identified.

KPMG LLP is a Delaware limited liability partnership,
the U.S. member firm of KPMG International Cooperative
("KPMG International"), a Swiss entity.

Purpose of this Report

The purpose of this report is solely to describe the scope of our testing of internal control and the result of that testing, and not to provide an opinion on the effectiveness of the Alcohol and Tobacco Tax and Trade Bureau's internal control. This report is an integral part of an audit performed in accordance with *Government Auditing Standards* in considering the Alcohol and Tobacco Tax and Trade Bureau's internal control. Accordingly, this communication is not suitable for any other purpose.

KPMG LLP

January 30, 2014

KPMG LLP
Suite 12000
1801 K Street, NW
Washington, DC 20006

Independent Auditors' Report on Compliance and Other Matters

Inspector General
United States Department of the Treasury

Administrator
Alcohol and Tobacco Tax and Trade Bureau:

We have audited, in accordance with auditing standards generally accepted in the United States of America; the standards applicable to financial audits contained in *Government Auditing Standards* issued by the Comptroller General of the United States; and Office of Management and Budget (OMB) Bulletin No. 14-02, *Audit Requirements for Federal Financial Statements*, the financial statements of Alcohol and Tobacco Tax and Trade Bureau, which comprise the balance sheets as of September 30, 2013 and 2012, and the related statements of net cost, changes in net position, budgetary resources, and custodial activity, for the years then ended, and the related notes to the financial statements, and have issued our report thereon dated January 30, 2014.

Compliance and Other Matters

As part of obtaining reasonable assurance about whether the Alcohol and Tobacco Tax and Trade Bureau's financial statements are free from material misstatement, we performed tests of its compliance with certain provisions of laws, regulations, and contracts, noncompliance with which could have a direct and material effect on the determination of financial statement amounts, and certain provisions of other laws and regulations specified in OMB Bulletin No. 14-02. However, providing an opinion on compliance with those provisions was not an objective of our audit, and accordingly, we do not express such an opinion. The results of our tests of compliance disclosed no instances of noncompliance or other matters that are required to be reported herein under *Government Auditing Standards* or OMB Bulletin No. 14-02.

Purpose of this Report

The purpose of this report is solely to describe the scope of our testing of compliance and the result of that testing, and not to provide an opinion on the Alcohol and Tobacco Tax and Trade Bureau's compliance. This report is an integral part of an audit performed in accordance with *Government Auditing Standards* in considering the Alcohol and Tobacco Tax and Trade Bureau's compliance. Accordingly, this communication is not suitable for any other purpose.

KPMG LLP

January 30, 2014

Page left intentionally blank.

ALCOHOL AND TOBACCO TAX AND TRADE BUREAU
BALANCE SHEETS
As of September 30, 2013 and 2012
(In Thousands)

	2013	2012
ASSETS		
Intragovernmental Assets:		
Fund Balance with Treasury (Note 2)	$32,142	$34,431
Accounts Receivable (Note 3)	541	262
Due from the General Fund (Notes 5 and 8)	3,739	2,873
Advances (Note 7)	460	751
Total Intragovernmental Assets	36,882	38,317
Accounts Receivable (Note 3)	417	444
Tax and Trade Receivables, Net (Notes 4 and 8)	16,868	20,334
Property, Plant and Equipment, Net (Note 6)	17,777	20,353
Advances	22	44
TOTAL ASSETS (Note 8)	$71,966	$79,492
LIABILITIES		
Intragovernmental Liabilities:		
Accounts Payable	$745	$480
Payroll Benefits	265	651
FECA Liabilities	31	39
Due to the General Fund (Notes 4 and 5)	13,661	18,851
Other Liabilities (Note 9)	3,207	1,483
Total Intragovernmental Liabilities	17,909	21,504
Accounts Payable	2,176	2,573
Payroll Benefits	1,095	2,723
FECA Actuarial Liability	206	228
Refunds	3,739	2,873
Unfunded Leave	4,202	4,233
Cash Bond Liabilities	11,167	12,570
Other Liabilities (Note 9)	1,345	560
TOTAL LIABILITIES	$41,839	$47,264
NET POSITION		
Unexpended Appropriations	$16,629	$16,377
Cumulative Results of Operations	13,498	15,851
TOTAL NET POSITION	$30,127	$32,228
TOTAL LIABILITIES AND NET POSITION	$71,966	$79,492

The accompanying notes are an integral part of these statements.

ALCOHOL AND TOBACCO TAX AND TRADE BUREAU
STATEMENTS OF NET COST
For the Years Ended September 30, 2013 and 2012
(In Thousands)

	2013	2012
COLLECT THE REVENUE		
Program Costs		
Intragovernmental Gross Costs	$14,216	$14,436
Less: Intragovernmental Earned Revenue	(2,601)	(1,308)
Intragovernmental Net Costs	11,615	13,128
Gross Costs with the Public	38,957	40,541
Less: Earned Revenues from the Public	(2,357)	(2,655)
Net Costs with the Public	36,600	37,886
Total Net Program Cost	$48,215	$51,014
PROTECT THE PUBLIC		
Program Costs		
Intragovernmental Gross Costs	$14,549	$13,988
Less: Intragovernmental Earned Revenue	(901)	(197)
Intragovernmental Net Costs	13,648	13,791
Gross Costs with the Public	39,870	39,285
Less: Earned Revenues from the Public	(817)	(401)
Net Costs with the Public	39,053	38,884
Total Net Program Cost	$52,701	$52,675
NET COST OF OPERATIONS (Note 13)	$100,916	$103,689

The accompanying notes are an integral part of these statements.

ALCOHOL AND TOBACCO TAX AND TRADE BUREAU
STATEMENTS OF CHANGES IN NET POSITION
For the Years Ended September 30, 2013 and 2012
(In Thousands)

	2013	2012
Cumulative Results of Operations		
Beginning Balances	$15,851	$15,817
Budgetary Financing Sources		
Appropriations Used	93,886	99,591
Other Financing Sources		
Transfers-in without reimbursement	693	91
Imputed Financing from Costs Absorbed		
by Others (Note 12)	3,984	4,041
Total Financing Sources	98,563	103,723
Net Cost of Operations (Note 13)	(100,916)	(103,689)
Net Change	(2,353)	34
Cumulative Results of Operations	$13,498	$15,851
UNEXPENDED APPROPRIATIONS		
Beginning Balances	$16,377	$16,559
Budgetary Financing Sources		
Appropriations Received	99,878	99,878
Other Adjustments	(5,740)	(469)
Appropriations Used	(93,886)	(99,591)
Total Budgetary Financing Sources	252	(182)
Net Position of Unexpended Appropriations	$16,629	$16,377
TOTAL NET POSITION	$30,127	$32,228

The accompanying notes are an integral part of these statements.

ALCOHOL AND TOBACCO TAX AND TRADE BUREAU
STATEMENTS OF BUDGETARY RESOURCES
For the Years Ended September 30, 2013 and 2012
(In Thousands)

	2013	2012
BUDGETARY RESOURCES (Note 14)		
Unobligated Balance Brought Forward, Oct 1	$3,116	$3,518
Recoveries of Prior Year Obligations	2,079	1,268
Other Changes in Unobligated Balance	(516)	(468)
Unobligated Balance from Prior Year Budget Authority, Net	4,679	4,318
Budget Authority:		
Appropriations	94,654	99,878
Spending Authority from Offsetting Collections	5,745	6,841
TOTAL BUDGETARY RESOURCES	105,078	111,037
STATUS OF BUDGETARY RESOURCES		
Obligations Incurred (Note 15)	$100,358	$107,921
Unobligated Balance Apportioned	845	398
Unobligated Balance Unapportioned	3,875	2,718
Total Unobligated Balance, End of Period	4,720	3,116
TOTAL STATUS OF BUDGETARY RESOURCES	$105,078	$111,037
CHANGE IN OBLIGATED BALANCE		
Unpaid Obligations Brought Forward, Oct 1	$21,795	$22,762
Obligations Incurred, Net (Note 15)	100,358	107,921
Outlays, Gross	(102,953)	(107,620)
Recoveries of Prior Year Unpaid Obligations, Actual	(2,079)	(1,268)
Unpaid Obligations , End of Period, Gross	17,121	21,795
Uncollected Payments Brought Forward, Federal Sources,		
Beginning of Period	(3,609)	(1,554)
Change in Uncollected Customer Payments, Federal Sources	1,398	(2,055)
Uncollected Payments, Federal Souces, End of Period	(2,211)	(3,609)
OBLIGATED BALANCE, END OF PERIOD, NET	$14,910	$18,186
BUDGET AUTHORITY AND OUTLAYS, NET		
Budget Authority:		
Budget Authority, Gross	$100,399	$106,719
Actual Offsetting Collections	(7,143)	(4,786)
Change in Uncollected Customer Payments, Federal Sources	1,398	(2,055)
BUDGET AUTHORITY, NET	$94,654	$99,878
Outlays:		
Outlays, Gross	102,953	107,620
Actual Offsetting Collections	(7,143)	(4,786)
Outlays, Net	95,810	102,834
Distributed Offsetting Receipts	(2)	(3)
AGENCY OUTLAYS, NET	$95,808	$102,831

The accompanying notes are an integral part of these statements.

ALCOHOL AND TOBACCO TAX AND TRADE BUREAU
STATEMENTS OF CUSTODIAL ACTIVITY
For the Years Ended September 30, 2013 and 2012
(In Thousands)

	2013	2012
SOURCES OF CUSTODIAL REVENUE		
Revenue Received		
Excise Taxes (Note 16)	$22,935,992	$23,378,944
Interest, Fines and Penalties	1,651	934
Other Custodial Revenue	2	3
Total Revenue Received (Note 17)	22,937,645	23,379,881
Refunds and Drawbacks (Note 16)	(380,961)	(323,447)
Net Revenue Received	22,556,684	23,056,434
Accrual Adjustment	(4,331)	15,176
Total Sources of Custodial Revenue	$22,552,353	$23,071,610
DISPOSITION OF CUSTODIAL REVENUE		
Amounts Provided to:		
General Fund	$21,436,310	$22,159,339
Fish and Wildlife Restoration Fund	762,651	511,385
Amounts Provided to Fund the		
Federal Government (Note 17)	22,198,961	22,670,724
Amounts Provided to Non-Federal		
Entities (Note 16)	357,723	385,710
Increases/(Decreases) in Amounts Yet		
to be Provided:		
General Fund	(5,190)	14,605
Fish and Wildlife Restoration Fund	1,724	1,420
(Increase)/Decrease in Accrued Refunds	(865)	(849)
Total Disposition of Custodial Revenue	$22,552,353	$23,071,610
NET CUSTODIAL REVENUE ACTIVITY	$ -	$ -

The accompanying notes are an integral part of these statements.

Notes to the Financial Statements

Note 1. Summary of Significant Accounting Policies

A. Reporting Entity

The Alcohol and Tobacco Tax and Trade Bureau (TTB) was established on January 24, 2003, as a result of the Homeland Security Act of 2002. The Act transferred firearms, explosives, and arson functions of the Bureau of Alcohol, Tobacco and Firearms (ATF) to the Department of Justice and retained the tax collection and consumer protection provisions of the Internal Revenue Code (IRC) and Federal Alcohol Administration Act in TTB within the Department of the Treasury. While the agency has a new name, the history of TTB's regulatory responsibility dates back to the creation of the Department of the Treasury and the first Federal taxes levied on distilled spirits in 1791. TTB has two primary programs: Collect the Revenue and Protect the Public. Under the Collect the Revenue program, TTB collects alcohol, tobacco, firearms, and ammunition excise taxes, and under its Protect the Public program, TTB protects the consumer by ensuring that alcohol beverages are labeled, advertised, and marketed in accordance with the law, and facilitates trade in beverage and industrial alcohols.

B. Basis of Presentation

The financial statements were prepared to report the significant assets, liabilities, and net cost of operations, changes in net position, budgetary resources, and custodial activities of TTB. The financial statements have been prepared from the books and records of TTB in conformity with generally accepted accounting principles (GAAP) in the United States, and form and content guidance for entity financial statements issued by the Office of Management and Budget (OMB) in OMB Circular A-136. TTB's accounting policies are summarized in this note. GAAP for Federal entities is prescribed by the Federal Accounting Standards Advisory Board (FASAB), which has been designated the official accounting standards-setting body for the Federal Government by the American Institute of Certified Public Accountants.

C. Basis of Accounting

Transactions are recorded on a proprietary accrual and a budgetary basis of accounting. Under the accrual basis, revenues are recorded when earned and expenses are recorded when incurred, regardless of when cash is exchanged. However, under the budgetary basis, funds availability is recorded based upon legal considerations and constraints. As a result, certain line items on the proprietary statements may not equal similar lines on the budgetary financial statements.

D. Revenue and Financing Sources

(1) Exchange Revenue

Exchange Revenues are inflows of resources to a Government entity that the entity has earned by providing something of value to the public or another Government entity at a price. The majority of the Exchange Revenues earned by the Bureau result from providing services to the Government of Puerto Rico, as well as other Treasury entities.

(2) Financing Sources

Financing sources provide inflows of resources during the reporting period and include appropriations used and imputed financing. Unexpended appropriations are recognized separately in determining net position, but are not financing sources until used. Imputed financing sources are the result of other Federal entities financing costs on behalf of TTB.

TTB receives the majority of the funding needed to support the Bureau through congressional appropriations. The appropriations received are annual and multi-year funding that may be used, within statutory limits, for operating and capital expenditures.

(3) Imputed Financing Sources

Imputed financing sources are the result of Federal entities financing costs on behalf of TTB. Those entities pay future benefits for health insurance, life insurance, and pension benefits for TTB employees.

E. Custodial Revenue

For TTB, most custodial revenues result from collecting taxes on alcohol and tobacco products, which are transferred to the General Fund, and recognized as a nonexchange revenue on the Federal government's consolidated financial statements. The excise taxes collected by TTB come from businesses, and the taxes are imposed and collected at the producer and importer levels of operations. Members of the regulated industries paying excise taxes are distilleries, breweries, bonded wineries, bonded wine cellars, manufacturers of cigarette tubes, manufacturers of tobacco products, and manufacturers and importers of firearms and ammunition. These taxes are recorded on the records on a modified cash basis of accounting. The Statement of Custodial Activity is presented on a net accrual basis.

F. Fund Balance with Treasury

The Fund Balance with Treasury is the undisbursed account balance with the Treasury, primarily resulting from undisbursed appropriations. The balance is available within statutory limits to pay current liabilities and finance authorized purchase obligations. The Fund Balance also includes a non-entity balance, primarily the result of custodial activities related to collecting escrow payments designed to finance Offers-in-Compromise and cash bonds held in lieu of corporate surety bonds guaranteeing payment of taxes.

G. Accounts Receivable

Intragovernmental accounts receivable consist of amounts due under reimbursable agreements with Federal entities for services provided by TTB. Public accounts receivable consist of taxes, penalties, and interest that have been assessed but unpaid at year end.

Receivables due from Federal agencies are considered to be fully collectible. An allowance for doubtful accounts is established for public receivables based on specific identification.

H. Property, Plant, and Equipment

Property, plant, and equipment purchased with a cost greater than or equal to $25,000 per unit and a useful life of two years or more, is capitalized and depreciated. Normal repairs and maintenance are charged to expense as incurred.

TTB also capitalizes internal use of software when the unit cost or development costs are greater than or equal to $25,000. The same threshold also applies to enhancements that add significant functionality to the software. TTB will amortize this software based on its classification. The classifications are as follows: 1) Enterprise and other business software (five years), and 2) Personal productivity and desktop operating software (three years).

Additionally, TTB also capitalizes like assets purchased in bulk when the unit price is greater than or equal to $5,000 and less than $25,000, with the aggregated purchase amount greater than or equal to $250,000.

Assets are depreciated on a straight-line basis beginning the month the asset was put in to use.

I. Advances

Advances are payments made to cover certain periodic expenses before those expenses are incurred. In accordance with Public Law 91-614, TTB participated in the Treasury's Working Capital Fund for which it receives services on a reimbursable basis. Payments from TTB to Treasury are made in advance and are authorized for services that have been deemed as more advantageous and more economical when provided centrally. The services provided include those for telecommunications, payroll/personnel systems, printing, and other centralized services. The amount reported represents the balance available at the end of the fiscal year after charges/expenses incurred by the fund are deducted.

J. Non-entity Assets

Non-entity assets consist primarily of cash and receivables for excise taxes and fees that are to be distributed to the Treasury, other Federal agencies, and other governments. Non-entity assets are not considered a financing source (revenue) available to offset the operating expenses of TTB.

K. Liabilities

Liabilities represent the amount of monies, or other resources, that are likely to be paid by TTB as the result of a transaction or event that has already occurred. However, no liability can be paid by TTB absent an appropriation. Liabilities for which an appropriation has not been enacted and for which there is uncertainty an appropriation will be enacted, are classified as a liability not covered by budgetary resources. Also, the Government, acting in its sovereign capacity, can abrogate liabilities of TTB that arise from other than contracts.

Intragovernmental liabilities consist of amounts payable to the Treasury for collections of excise tax, fees receivable, payments to other Federal agencies, and accrued Federal Employees' Compensation Act (FECA) charges. Liabilities also include amounts due to be refunded to taxpayers, as well as amounts held in escrow for Offers-in-Compromise and cash bonds held in guaranteeing payment of taxes.

L. Litigation Contingencies and Settlements

Probable and estimable litigation and claims against TTB are recognized as a liability and expense for the full amount of the expected loss. Expected litigation and claim losses include settlements to be paid from the Treasury Judgment Fund (Judgment Fund) on behalf of TTB and settlements to be paid from Bureau appropriations. The Judgment Fund pays Bivens-type tort claims. Settlements paid from the Judgment Fund for TTB are recognized as an expense and imputed financing source.

M. Annual, Sick, and Other Leave

Annual and compensatory leave earned by TTB employees, but not yet used, is reported as an accrued liability. The accrued balance is adjusted annually to current pay rates. Any portions of the accrued leave, for which funding is not available, are recorded as an unfunded liability. Sick and other leave are expensed as taken.

N. Interest on Late Payments

Pursuant to the prompt payment Act, 31 # U.S.C. & 3901-3907, Federal agencies must pay interest on payments for goods or services made to business concerns after their due date. The due date is generally 30 days after receipt of a proper invoice or acceptance of the goods or services.

O. Retirement Plan

Employees hired after December 31, 1983, are automatically covered by FERS and Social Security. For most employees hired after December 31, 1983, TTB also contributes the employers' matching share of Social Security. For the FERS basic benefit, employees contribute 0.8 to 3.1 percent of basic pay while TTB contributes 11.9 percent, for a total contribution rate of 12.7 to 15.0 percent in FY 2013. The employee contribution is an increase over the .8 percent contributed in FY 2012. The cost of providing a FERS basic benefit, as provided by the Office of Personnel Management (OPM), is equal to the amounts contributed by TTB and the employees.

All employees are eligible to contribute to the Thrift Savings Plan (TSP). For those employees participating in the FERS, a TSP account is automatically established and TTB makes a mandatory 1 percent contribution to this account. In addition, TTB makes matching contributions, ranging from 1 to 4 percent, for FERS-eligible employees who contribute to their TSP accounts. Matching contributions are not made to the TSP accounts established by CSRS employees.

TTB recognized the full cost of providing future pension and other retirement benefits (ORB) for current employees as required by Statement of Federal Financial Accounting Standards (SFFAS) No. 5. Full cost includes pension and ORB contributions paid out of Bureau appropriations and costs financed by OPM. Costs financed by OPM are reported in the accompanying financial statements as an imputed financing revenue source. Reporting amounts such as plan assets, accumulated plan benefits, or unfunded liabilities, if any, is the responsibility of OPM.

P. Federal Employees' Compensation Act

The Federal Employees' Compensation Act (FECA) provides income and medical cost protection to covered Federal civilian employees injured on the job and employees who have incurred a work-related injury or occupational disease. The future workers' compensation estimates were generated from an application of actuarial procedures developed to estimate the liability for FECA benefits. The actuarial liability estimates for FECA benefits include the expected liability for death, disability, medical, and miscellaneous costs for approved compensation cases. The liability is determined using the paid losses extrapolation method, which is calculated over the next 37-year period. This method utilizes historical benefit patterns related to a specific incurred period to predict ultimate payments related to that period.

Claims are paid for TTB employees by the Department of Labor (DOL) from the FECA fund, for which TTB reimburses DOL. The accrued liability represents claims paid by DOL for TTB employees, for which the fund has not been reimbursed. The actuarial liability is an estimate of future costs to be paid on claims made by TTB employees. The estimated future cost is not obligated against budgetary resources until the year in which the cost is billed to TTB.

Q. Use of Estimates

The preparation of financial statements requires management to make estimates and assumptions that affect the reported amount of assets and liabilities, as well as the disclosure of contingent liabilities at the date of the financial statements, and the amount of revenues and cost reported during the period. Actual results could differ from those estimates.

R. Tax Exempt Status

As an agency of the Federal Government, TTB is exempt from all income taxes imposed by any governing body, whether it is a Federal, state, commonwealth, local, or foreign government.

S. Changes in Presentation

The FY2012 financial statements were reclassified to conform to the FY2013 financial statements presentations requirements. The reclassifications had no material effect on total assets, liabilities, net position, changed in net position, budgetary resources or custodial activity as previously reported.

T. Subsequent Events

Subsequent events and transaction occurring after September 30, 2013 through the date of the auditors' opinion have been evaluated for potential recognition or disclosure in the financial statements. The date of the auditors' opinion also represents the date that the financial statements were available for issue.

Note 2. Fund Balance with Treasury

Fund Balance with Treasury as of September 30, 2013 and 2012 consisted of the following (in thousands):

	2013	2012
Fund Balances:		
General Funds	$19,630	$21,302
Other Funds	12,512	13,129
Total	$32,142	$34,431
Status of Fund Balances:		
Unobligated Balance - Available	$845	$398
Unobligated Balance - Unavailable	3,875	2,718
Obligated Balance Not Yet Disbursed	14,910	18,186
Subtotal	19,630	21,302
Adjustment for Non-Budgetary Funds	12,512	13,129
Total Status of Fund Balances	$32,142	$34,431

The other funds and non-budgetary fund balance primarily represents cash bonds, which are cash payments made to the Bureau by taxpayers, in lieu of obtaining corporate surety bonds, guaranteeing payment of taxes. It also includes Offers-in-Compromise (OIC). OICs are payments made to the Bureau, being held in escrow, to finance offers from taxpayers to settle their tax debt at less than the assessed amount.

The unobligated balance that is unavailable is the balance of prior years' expired appropriations.

Note 3. Accounts Receivable

Accounts Receivable as of September 30, 2013 and 2012 consisted of the following (in thousands):

	2013	2012
Intragovernmental Accounts Receivable:		
Due from Treasury Executive Office of Asset Forfieture	$86	$68
Due from Community Financial Development Institutions Fund	455	194
Total Intragovernmental Accounts Receivable	$541	$262
Due from the Government of Puerto Rico	$414	$436
Due from Employees	3	8
Total Accounts Receivable Due from the Public	$417	$444

No allowance for doubtful accounts has been recognized, nor have any accounts been written off. All intragovernmental accounts receivable are considered fully collectible. Additionally, other non-Federal receivables consist of a receivable from the government of Puerto Rico, which is collected via an offset to cover-over payments the Bureau remits to Puerto Rico, and employee accounts receivable, which can be collected via salary offsets.

Note 4. Tax and Trade Receivables, Net

Tax and Trade Receivables as of September 30, 2013 and 2012 consisted of the following (in thousands):

	2013	2012
Tax and Trade Receivables	$87,086	$59,965
Interest Receivable	7,805	5,019
Penalties, Fines and Administrative Fees Receivable	23,457	15,490
Total Tax and Trade Receivables	118,348	80,474
Allowance for Doubtful Accounts	(101,480)	(60,140)
Total Tax and Trade Receivables, Net	$16,868	$20,334

All tax and trade receivables are non-entity assets. An allowance for uncollectible amounts has been established based on: 1) an analysis of individual receivable balances and 2) the application of historical non-collection rates for similar types of receivables. Because current laws governing the collection period for these tax assessments, 26 U.S.C. 6502, stipulate taxes are collectible for 10 years from the date the taxes were assessed, a large amount of aged receivables that are not likely to be collected have been offset with an allowance, but not written off. This is an offsetting liability reported as Due to the General Fund.

The increase in gross receivables is largely related to new receivables with one taxpayer, approximating $25 million. The remaining $13 million increase is primarily related to six taxpayers who's receivables increased between $1.3 - $3.3 million.

Note 5. Due from the General Fund and Due to the General Fund

In addition to collecting taxes from the alcohol and tobacco industries, the Bureau also is responsible for paying refunds, when applicable, to those same industry members. Amounts due from the General Fund represent a receivable from appropriations to cover the Bureau's accrued refund liability to alcohol and tobacco excise taxpayers.

	2013	2012
Due from the General Fund (in thousands)	$3,739	$2,873

Amounts due to the General Fund primarily represent the balance of receivables related to Alcohol and Tobacco excise taxes. Receivables related to Firearms and Ammunition excise taxes are payable to the Department of Interior's Fish and Wildlife Restoration Fund, not the General Fund.

	2013	2012
Due to the General Fund (in thousands)	$13,661	$18,851

Note 6. Property, Plant, and Equipment, Net (PP&E)

Property, Plant and Equipment as of September 30, 2013 and 2012 consisted of the following (in thousands):

2013	Estimated Useful Life (Years)	Acquisition Value	Accumulated Depreciation	Net Book Value
Internal Use Software	3 - 5	$13,644	$7,523	$6,121
Equipment	4 - 6	11,611	7,593	4,018
Leasehold Improvements	2 - 5	1,312	1,090	222
Building	40	9,772	2,356	7,416
Total PP&E		$36,339	$18,562	$17,777

2012	Estimated Useful Life (Years)	Acquisition Value	Accumulated Depreciation	Net Book Value
Internal Use Software	3 - 5	$13,644	$5,542	$8,102
Equipment	4 - 6	11,064	6,792	4,272
Leasehold Improvements	2 - 5	1,134	825	309
Building	40	9,772	2,102	7,670
Total PP&E		$35,614	$15,261	$20,353

Depreciation and amortization are calculated using the straight-line method.

The balance in the buildings account represents TTB's 13.2 percent equity interest in the National Laboratory Center facility in Beltsville, Maryland, which TTB co-owns with ATF.

Note 7. Advances

Intragovernmental advances consist of the balances paid to Treasury's Working Capital Fund that have not yet been earned and billed by the fund. Advances with the public generally consist of prepaid services agreements for support or maintenance.

Note 8. Non-entity Assets

Non-entity Assets as of September 30, 2013 and 2012 consisted of the following (in thousands):

	2013	2012
Intragovernmental Non-entity Assets:		
Fund Balance with Treasury	$12,512	$13,129
Due from the General Fund	3,739	2,873
Total Intragovernmental Non-entity Assets	16,251	16,002
Tax and Trade Receivables, Net	16,868	20,334
Total Non-Entity Assets	33,119	36,336
Total Entity Assets	38,847	43,156
Total Assets	$71,966	$79,492

Note 9. Other Liabilities

Other Liabilities as of September 30, 2013 and 2012 consisted of the following (in thousands):

	2013	2012
Due to the Fish and Wildlife Fund	$3,207	$1,483
Other Intragovernmental Liabilities	3,207	1,483
Offers-in-Compromise not yet Accepted	1,345	560
Total Other Liabilities with the Public	1,345	560
Total Other Liabilities	$4,552	$2,043

All Other Liabilities are considered current liabilities.

Note 10. Liabilities Not Covered by Budgetary Resources

Liabilities not Covered by Budgetary Resources as of September 30, 2013 and 2012 consisted of the following (in thousands):

	2013	2012
Accrued FECA Liability	$31	$39
Total Intragovernmental Liabilities not Covered by Budgetary Resources	31	39
FECA Actuarial Liability	206	228
Accrued Leave	4,202	4,233
Total Liabilities with the Public not Covered by Budgetary Resources	4,408	4,461
Total Liabilities not Covered By Budgetary Resouces	4,439	4,500
Total Liabilities Covered by Budgetary Resources	37,400	42,764
Total Liabilities	$41,839	$47,264

Note 11. Future Funding Requirements

Total liabilities not covered by budgetary resources generally do not equal the total financing sources yet to be provided on the Reconciliation of Net Cost of Operations to Budget. The amounts reported on the Balance Sheet are period ending balances, while the amounts reported on the Reconciliation of Net Cost of Operations to Budget are activity for the period.

Generally, liabilities not covered by budgetary resources require future funding and can be liquidated only with the enactment of future appropriations.

Note 12. Imputed Financing

Imputed Financing as of September 30, 2013 and 2012 consisted of the following (in thousands):

	2013	2012
Health Insurance	$2,146	$2,440
Life Insurance	8	8
Pension	1,830	1,593
Total Imputed Financing	$3,984	$4,041

Imputed financing recognizes actual cost of future benefits to be paid by other Federal entities. These benefits include Federal Employees Health and Benefits Program (FEHB), Federal Employees Group Life Insurance Program (FEGLI), and pensions. Imputed financing also recognizes costs paid by the Judgment Fund. The Fund was established and funded by Congress under 31 U.S.C. 1304 to pay in whole or in part court judgments and settlement agreements negotiated by Treasury on behalf of agencies, as well as certain types of administrative awards. The Judgment Fund did not pay out any awards on TTB's behalf during fiscal years 2013 or 2012.

TTB does not report CSRS assets, FERS assets, accumulated plan benefits, or unfunded liabilities, if any, applicable to retirement plans because the accounting for and reporting of such amounts is the responsibility of OPM. Based on cost factors provided by OPM, which vary by retirement plan, estimated future pension benefits for TTB employees, to be paid by OPM, totaled $1.8 million and $1.6 million for fiscal years 2013 and 2012 respectively. Similarly, OPM rather than TTB, reports liabilities for future payments to retired employees who participate in the FEHB and FEGLI programs. The FEHB cost factor applied to a weighted average number of employees enrolled in the FEHB program decreased in FY 2013 to $5,190 from $5,817 in FY 2012, producing $2.1 million and $2.4 million of imputed cost for employees' health benefits in each respective year. The cost factor, as provided by OPM, for employees enrolled in the FEGLI program, remained unchanged from FY 2012 to FY 2013, at .02 percent of employees' basic pay. The FEGLI amounts, approximating $8,000 each year, are also included as an expense and imputed financing source in TTB financial statements for fiscal years 2013 and 2012, respectively.

Note 13. Consolidated Gross Cost and Earned Revenue by Budget Functional Classification

Consolidated Gross Cost and Earned Revenue by Budget Function Classification as of September 30, 2013 and 2012 consisted of the following (in thousands):

Fiscal Year Ended September 30, 2013

Activity	Budget Function Classification (BFC)	BFC Code	Gross Costs	Earned Revenue	Net Costs
Intragovernmental	Central Fiscal Operations	803	$28,765	$(3,502)	$25,263
With the Public	Central Fiscal Operations	803	78,827	(3,174)	75,653
Consolidated	Central Fiscal Operations	803	$107,592	$(6,676)	$100,916

Fiscal Year Ended September 30, 2012

Activity	Budget Function Classification (BFC)	BFC Code	Gross Costs	Earned Revenue	Net Costs
Intragovernmental	Central Fiscal Operations	803	$28,424	$(1,505)	$26,919
With the Public	Central Fiscal Operations	803	79,826	(3,056)	76,770
Consolidated	Central Fiscal Operations	803	$108,250	$(4,561)	$103,689

Note 14. Statement of Budgetary Resources vs. Budget of the United States Government

The following chart displays balances from the FY 2012 Statement of Budgetary Resources and actual fiscal year balances included in the FY 2014 President's Budget. There were no differences. The FY 2015 budget, which would include FY 2013 actuals, had not been published at the time of this report.

Fiscal Year Ended September 30, 2012 (In Millions / Unaudited)	Statement of Budgetary Resources	President's Budget
Budgetary Resources:		
Appropriations	$100	$100
Spending Authority from Offsetting Collections	7	7
Budgetary Resources Available for Obligation	$107	$107
Change in Obligated Balances:		
Unpaid Obligations brought forward, Beginning of Period	$23	$23
Obligations Incurred	108	108
Outlays, Gross	(108)	(108)
Recoveries of Prior Year Unpaid Obligations	(1)	(1)
Unpaid Obligations, End of Period	$22	$22
Uncollected Payments, Federal Sources, End of Period	(4)	(4)
Obligated Balance, End of Period	$18	$18
Outlays:		
Outlays, Gross	$108	$108
Actaul Offsetting Collections	(5)	(5)
Outlays, Net	$103	$103

Additionally, the FY 2014 President's Budget disclosed budget authority of $376 million for FY 2012, funding cover-over payments to Puerto Rico, which is not reported in the Statement of Budgetary Resources.

The cover-over payments and associated tax revenues are reported as custodial activity of the Bureau. The tax revenues are not available for use in the operation of the Bureau and are not reported on the Statement of Net Cost. Likewise, the resultant cover-over payments are not recognized as an operating expense of the Bureau. Consequently, to present the refunds as an expense of the Bureau on the Statement of Net Cost would be inconsistent with the reporting of the related Federal tax revenue and would materially distort the costs incurred by the Bureau in meeting its strategic objectives. Further, since this activity is not reported on the Statement of Net Cost, it would be contradictory to report the budget authority on the Statement of Budgetary Resources.

Note 15. Apportionment Categories of Obligations Incurred

Obligations Incurred as of September 30, 2013 and 2012 consisted of the following (in thousands):

Fiscal Year	Apportionment Category	Direct Obligations	Reimbursable Obligations	Total Obligations Incurred
2013	Category B	$94,939	$5,419	$100,358
2012	Category B	$100,769	$7,152	$107,921

The amount of direct and reimbursable obligations against amounts apportioned under Category B is reported in the table above. Apportionment categories are determined by the apportionment categories reported on the Standard Form 132 *Apportionment and Reapportionment Schedule*. Category B represents annual apportionments.

	2013	2012
Undelivered Orders, End of Period	$13,322	$16,185

Note 16. Net Custodial Revenue Activity

- **Excise Taxes**

  As an agent of the Federal Government and as authorized by 26 U.S.C., TTB collects excise taxes from alcohol, tobacco, firearms, and ammunition industries. In addition, special occupational taxes are collected from certain alcohol and tobacco businesses. During FY 2013 and FY 2012, TTB collected $22.9 billion and $23.4 billion respectively in taxes, interest, and other custodial revenues.

  Substantially all of the taxes collected by TTB net of related refund disbursements are remitted to the Department of Treasury General Fund. The Department of Treasury further distributes this revenue to Federal agencies in accordance with various laws and regulations. The firearms and ammunition excise taxes are an exception. Those revenues are remitted to the Fish and Wildlife Restoration Fund under provisions of the Pittman-Robertson Act of 1937.

- **Refunds and Other Payments**

  During FY 2013 and FY 2012, TTB issued $739 million and $709 million in refunds, cover-over payments, and drawback payments in the respective years.

Tax Refunds

Tax Refunds result when taxpayers file returns for payments made for a given tax period and the result of the return is an overpayment.

Cover-over Payments

Federal excise taxes are collected under the Internal Revenue Code of 1986, 26 U.S.C., on certain articles produced in Puerto Rico and the Virgin Islands, and imported into the United States. In accordance with 26 U.S.C. 7652, such taxes collected on rum imported into the United States are custodial revenues and "covered over," or paid into, the treasuries of Puerto Rico and the Virgin Islands.

TTB maintains operations in Puerto Rico to enforce the provisions of chapter 51 in respect to items of Puerto Rican manufacture brought in to the United States. These operations include conducting annual revenue, application, and product integrity investigations of large alcohol and tobacco industry members. Except for application investigations, TTB investigates medium and small alcohol and tobacco producers in response to specific problems and risk indicators. Revenue inspections are used to verify that TTB is collecting all of the revenue that is rightfully due from the taxpayer. TTB staff in Puerto Rico also conducts qualification inspections of all distilled spirits producers/processors, wineries, wholesalers, importers, Manufacturer of Nonbeverage Products (MNBP) claimants, and Specially Denatured Alcohol permit applicants. All costs associated with the functioning and supporting of the Puerto Rico office, $3.2 and $3.1 million in FY 2013 and FY 2012 respectively, are offset against the cover-over payments made by the United States to Puerto Rico.

Drawbacks

Under current law, 26 U.S.C. 5134, MNBP permittees may be eligible to claim a refund of tax paid on distilled spirits used in their products. In the case of distilled spirits, on which the tax has been paid or determined, a drawback shall be allowed on each proof gallon at the rate of $1 less than the rate at which the distilled spirits tax had been paid or determined. The refund is due upon the claimant providing evidence that the distilled spirits on which the tax has been paid or determined were unfit for beverage purposes and were used in the manufacture or production of medicines, medicinal preparations, food products, flavors, flavoring extracts, or perfume.

Refunds, Drawbacks and Cover-over Payments as of September 30, 2013 and 2012 consisted of the following (in thousands):

	2013	2012
Alcohol and Tobacco Excise Tax Refunds	$35,278	$30,293
Drawbacks on MNBP Claims	345,231	289,330
Interest and Other Payments	452	3,824
Refunds and Drawbacks	380,961	323,447
Cover-over Payments - Puerto Rico	349,017	376,373
Cover-over Payments - Virgin Islands	8,706	9,337
Amounts Provided to Non-federal Entities	357,723	385,710
Total Refunds, Drawbacks and Coverover Payments	$738,684	$709,157

Note 17. Custodial Revenue

Collection and Disposition of Custodial Revenue as of September 30, 2013 and 2012 consisted of the following (in thousands):

FY 2013 Collections and Refunds by Tax Year

Revenue Type	2013	2012	2011	Pre-2011	FY 2013 Total
Excise Taxes	$16,718,436	$6,213,206	$1,457	$2,893	$22,935,992
Fines, Penalties, Interest and Other	161	1,247	62	183	1,653
Total Revenue Received	16,718,597	6,214,453	1,519	3,076	22,937,645
Less: Amounts Collected for Non-federal Entities	(357,723)	-	-	-	(357,723)
Total	$16,360,874	$6,214,453	$1,519	$3,076	$22,579,922

Refund Type	2013	2012	2011	Pre-2011	FY 2013 Total
Excise Taxes	$190,370	$185,272	$4,767	$278	$380,687
Fines, Penalties, Interest and Other	12	51	191	20	274
Total Refunds & Drawbacks	$190,382	$185,323	$4,958	$298	$380,961
Amounts Provided to Fund the Federal Government	$16,170,492	$6,029,130	$(3,439)	$2,778	$22,198,961

FY 2012 Collections and Refunds by Tax Year

Revenue Type	2012	2011	2010	Pre-2010	FY 2012 Total
Excise Taxes	$17,158,574	$6,209,558	$3,510	$7,302	$23,378,944
Fines, Penalties, Interest and Other	246	371	184	136	937
Total Revenue Received	17,158,820	6,209,929	3,694	7,438	23,379,881
Less: Amounts Collected for Non-federal Entities	(385,710)	-	-	-	(385,710)
Total	$16,773,110	$6,209,929	$3,694	$7,438	$22,994,171
Refund Type					
Excise Taxes	$159,021	$155,721	$1,011	$7,107	$322,860
Fines, Penalties, Interest and Other	587	-	-	-	587
Total Refunds & Drawbacks	$159,608	$155,721	$1,011	$7,107	$323,447
Amounts Provided to Fund the Federal Government	$16,613,502	$6,054,208	$2,683	$331	$22,670,724

Note 18. Reconciliation of Net Cost of Operations to Budget

The Reconciliation of Net Cost of Operations to Budget explains the difference between the budgetary net obligations and the proprietary net cost of operations.

Reconciliation of Net Cost of Operations to Budget, as of September 30, 2013 and 2012 consisted of the following (in thousands):

	2013	2012
Resources Used to Finance Activities		
Budgetary Resources Obligated		
Obligations Incurred	$100,358	$107,921
Less: Spending Authority from Offsetting Collections and Recoveries	(7,824)	(8,109)
Obligations Net of Offsetting Collections and Recoveries	92,534	99,812
Less: Offsetting Receipts	(2)	(3)
Net Obligations	92,532	99,809
Other Resources		
Transfers-in without Reimbursement	693	91
Imputed Financing from Costs Absorbed by Others	3,984	4,041
Net Other Resources Used to Finance Activities	4,677	4,132
Total Resources Used to Finance Activities	$97,209	$103,941

	2013	2012
Resources Used to Finance Items not Part of the Net Cost Of Operations		
Change in Budgetary Resources Obligated for Goods, Services and Benefits Ordered but not Yet Provided (+/-)	$(1,206)	$181
Resources that Fund Expenses Recognized in Prior Periods	55	193
Other Budgetary Offsetting Collections and Receipts that do not Affect Net Cost of Operations	691	88
Resources that Finance the Acquisition of Assets	1,787	3,625
Other Resources or Adjustments to Net Obligated Resources that do not Affect Net Cost of Operations (+/-)	(693)	(91)
Total Resources Used to Finance Items not Part of the Net Cost of Operations	634	3,996
Total Resources Used to Finance the Net Cost of Operations	$96,575	$99,945
Components of the Net Cost of Operations Requiring or Generating Resources in Future Periods		
Components Requiring or Generating Resources in Future Periods:		
Other (+/-)	$ -	$ -
Total Components of Net Cost of Operations that will Require or Generate Resources in Future Periods	$ -	$ -
Components of the Net Cost of Operations not Requiring or Generating Resources		
Depreciation and Amortization	$4,286	$3,744
Revaluation of Assets or Liabilities	55	-
Total Components of Net Cost of Operations that will not Require or Generate Resources	$4,341	$3,744
Total Components of Net Cost of Operations that will not Require or Generate Resources in the Current Period	$4,341	$3,744
NET COST OF OPERATIONS	$100,916	$103,689

Note 19: Contingent Liabilities

As of September 30, 2013, TTB is not party to any legal matters where the estimated loss would be of a material amount.

Required Supplementary Information (Unaudited)

Budgetary Information

Budgetary information aggregated for the purposes of the Statement of Budgetary Resources should be disaggregated for each of an entity's major budget accounts (i.e., Appropriated Funds, Trust Funds, Revolving Funds, or other funds) and presented as Supplementary Information. However, for proprietary reporting, TTB only has appropriated funds. Consequently, a Combining Statement of Budgetary Resources disaggregated by fund type has not been presented.

Excise Tax and Other Collections

Required Supplementary Information
Excise Tax and Other Collections by Fiscal Year
Unaudited (In Thousands)

Fiscal Year	Alcohol	Tobacco	FAET	SOT	FST	Other	Total
2004	$6,995,366	$7,433,852	$216,006	$100,562	$ -	$359	$14,746,145
2005	7,074,076	7,409,608	225,818	10,190	9	141	14,719,842
2006	7,182,940	7,350,058	249,578	2,895	638	146	14,786,255
2007	7,232,138	7,194,081	287,835	2,808	-	32	14,716,894
2008	7,420,576	6,851,705	312,622	448	-	634	14,585,985
2009	7,424,292	11,548,504	452,693	272	1,192,375	970	20,619,106
2010	7,476,789	15,913,479	360,813	300	8,558	180	23,760,119
2011	7,594,330	15,515,073	344,262	268	5,220	2,257	23,461,410
2012	7,856,391	15,002,616	514,622	249	5,942	61	23,379,881
2013	7,851,953	14,321,017	762,836	280	1,521	38	22,937,645
Average	$7,410,885	$10,853,999	$372,709	$11,827	$121,426	$482	$18,771,328

FAET – Firearms and Ammunition Excise Tax

SOT – Special Occupational Tax

FST – Floor Stocks Tax

The sharp decrease in SOT tax collections was the result of a new law that became effective during fiscal year 2005 that suspended the collection of most of the taxes. The law became permanent in 2008.

TTB collects FAET taxes on behalf of the Department of Interior, U.S. Fish and Wildlife Service, and deposits the collections directly into the Fish and Wildlife Restoration Fund. During fiscal years 2013 and 2012, TTB incurred $1.8 million and $1.7 million respectively of direct and indirect costs associated with collecting the FAET taxes. The law currently does not provide for TTB to recover these costs. The cost of the program was communicated to the U.S. Fish and Wildlife Service so the agency could properly record an imputed cost in its financial records.

Refunds, Cover-over Payments, and Drawback Payments

Required Supplementary Information
Refunds, Cover-over Payments and Drawback Payments by Fiscal Year
Unaudited (In Thousands)

Fiscal Year	Cover-over Puerto Rico	Cover-over Virgin Islands	A&T Excise Tax	Drawbacks MNBP Claims	Interest and Other	Total
2004	$335,293	$6,244	$15,409	$355,605	$1,216	$713,767
2005	419,602	6,010	18,504	317,132	2,100	763,348
2006	358,664	6,491	17,524	337,632	699	721,010
2007	459,278	8,054	13,208	335,706	972	817,218
2008	373,418	7,615	14,125	283,462	2,938	681,558
2009	472,695	8,624	17,791	268,612	252	767,974
2010	378,186	8,871	28,232	297,596	315	713,200
2011	452,040	9,592	33,414	306,584	418	802,048
2012	376,373	9,337	30,293	289,330	3,824	709,157
2013	349,017	8,706	35,278	345,231	452	738,684
Average	$397,457	$7,954	$22,378	$313,689	$1,319	$742,796

A&T – Alcohol and Tobacco

MNBP – Manufacturer of Nonbeverage Products

Note – During January 2013, the Puerto Rico cover-over rate was increased from $10.50 per proof gallon to $13.25 per proof gallon, with retroactive provisions, as it has every two years over the last ten years. The increased rate expires December 31, 2013. Despite the increase in the cover-over rate, an overall decrease in cover-over payments to Puerto Rico resulted primarily because of Diageo moving its operations from Puerto Rico to the Virgin Islands.

Other Information (Unaudited)

Other Information
Schedule of Spending
For the Years Ended September 30, 2013 and 2012
Unaudited (In Thousands)

	2013	2012
What Money is Available to Spend		
Total Resources	$105,078	$111,037
Less: Amount Available but not Agreed to be Spent	(845)	(398)
Less: Amount Not Available to Be Spent	(3,875)	(2,718)
Total Amounts Agreed to be Spent	$100,358	$107,921
How was the Money Spent		
Collect the Revenue		
Object Class 11: Personnel Compensation	$24,284	$23,722
Object Class 12: Personnel Benefits	7,098	6,730
Object Class 21: Travel	1,334	1,757
Object Class 23: Rent, Utilities, and Telecommunications Services	3,018	3,475
Object Class 25: Contractual Services	14,858	15,878
Object Class 31: Equipment and Software	2,145	3,255
Other	471	713
Total Collect the Revenue	53,208	55,530
Protect the Public		
Object Class 11: Personnel Compensation	24,164	22,998
Object Class 12: Personnel Benefits	6,898	6,330
Object Class 21: Travel	516	634
Object Class 23: Rent, Utilities, and Telecommunications Services	2,841	3,273
Object Class 25: Contractual Services	13,668	14,734
Object Class 31: Equipment and Software	1,344	3,556
Other	314	565
Total Protect the Public	49,745	52,090
Total Spending	102,953	107,620
Change in Amounts Remaining to be Spent	(2,595)	301
Total Amounts Agreed to be Spent	$100,358	$107,921

Intragovernmental Assets

Other Information
Intragovernmental Assets
As of September 30, 2013
Unaudited (In Thousands)

Trading Partner	Agency Code	Fund Balance W/ Treasury	Accounts Receivable	Advances
Department of the Treasury	20	$ -	$541	$460
General Fund	99	32,142	3,739	-
Total		$32,142	$4,280	$460

Other Information
Intragovernmental Assets
As of September 30, 2012
Unaudited (In Thousands)

Trading Partner	Agency Code	Fund Balance W/ Treasury	Accounts Receivable	Advances
Department of the Treasury	20	$ -	$262	$751
General Fund	99	34,431	2,873	-
Total		$34,431	$3,135	$751

Intragovernmental Liabilities

Other Information
Intragovernmental Liabilities
As of September 30, 2013
Unaudited (In Thousands)

Trading Partner	Agency Code	Accounts Payable	Accrued FECA	Custodial and Other Liabilities
Government Printing Office	04	$108	$ -	$ -
Department of the Interior	14	-	-	3,207
Department of Justice	15	469	-	-
Department of Labor	16	-	31	-
Office of Personnel Management	24	-	-	196
General Services Administration	47	168	-	-
Treasury General Fund	99	-	-	13,730
Total		$745	$31	$17,133

Other Information
Intragovernmental Liabilities
As of September 30, 2012
Unaudited (In Thousands)

Trading Partner	Agency Code	Accounts Payable	Accrued FECA	Custodial and Other Liabilities
Government Printing Office	04	$26	$ -	$ -
Department of the Interior	14	-	-	1,483
Department of Justice	15	330	-	-
Department of Labor	16	-	39	-
Office of Personnel Management	24	-	-	480
General Services Administration	47	123	-	-
Treasury General Fund	99	1	-	19,022
Total		$480	$39	$20,985

Intragovernmental Earned Revenue

Other Information
Intragovernmental Earned Revenue
For the Fiscal Years Ended September 30, 2013 and 2012
Unaudited (In Thousands)

Trading Partner	Agency Code	2013	2012
Department of Treasury	20	$3,502	$1,500
Department of Justice	15	-	5
Total		$3,502	$1,505

Budget Function Classification (BFC)	BFC Code	2013	2012
Central Fiscal Operations	803	$3,502	$1,505
Total		$3,502	$1,505

Intragovernmental Gross Cost

Other Information
Intragovernmental Gross Cost
For the Fiscal Years Ended September 30, 2013 and 2012
Unaudited (In Thousands)

Trading Partner	Agency Code	2013	2012
Library of Congress	03	$71	$68
Government Printing Office	04	232	160
Department of Interior	14	-	75
Department of Justice	15	1,066	742
Department of Labor	16	8	19
United States Postal Services	18	44	54
Department of State	19	-	1
Department of the Treasury	20	5,573	5,247
Office of Personnel Management	24	12,795	12,480
General Services Administration	47	5,480	6,020
Environmental Protection Agency	68	4	20
Department of Homeland Security	70	324	450
Department of Health and Human Services	75	22	49
National Archives Records Administration	88	39	42
Department of Defense	97	119	100
General Fund	99	2,988	2,897
Total		$28,765	$28,424

During fiscal years 2013 and 2012, TTB incurred costs with other Federal agencies totaling approximately $28.8 million and $28.4 million, in each year respectively. The majority of those costs were associated with the five entities detailed below.

- **Department of Justice:** TTB paid ATF $1.1 million and $742,000 in fiscal years 2013 and 2012 respectively for shared lab space and shared building services.

- **Department of the Treasury:** The Bureau received services from Treasury's Working Capital Fund, as well as administrative services from the Bureau of Public Debt's Administrative Resource Center, in fiscal years 2013 and 2012 in the amounts of $5.6 million and $5.2 million respectively.

- **Office of Personnel Management:** TTB incurred $12.8 million and $12.5 million in costs for employee benefits for fiscal years 2013 and 2012 respectively.

- **General Services Administration:** TTB paid $5.5 million and $6.0 million to GSA for rent and information technology services in fiscal years 2013 and 2012 respectively.

- **General Fund:** The Bureau paid $3.0 and $2.9 million in fiscal years 2013 and 2012 respectively for employee benefits and lockbox fees.

Part IV: Appendices

Principal Officers of TTB

Administrator . . . . John Manfreda

Deputy Administrator . . . . Mary Ryan

Equal Employment Opportunity and Diversity Advancement . . . . Tiara Ngo

Assistant Administrator, Field Operations . . . . Tom Crone

Assistant Administrator, Headquarters Operations . . . . Theresa McCarthy

Assistant Administrator, Management/CFO . . . . Cheri Mitchell

Assistant Administrator, Information Resources/CIO . . . . Robert Hughes

Executive Liaison for Industry and State Matters . . . . Susan Evans

Chief Counsel . . . . Anthony Gledhill

For additional information, contact:

Alcohol and Tobacco Tax and Trade Bureau

1310 G Street, NW, Box 12

Washington, DC 20005

(202) 453-2000

http://www.ttb.gov

TTB Organization Chart

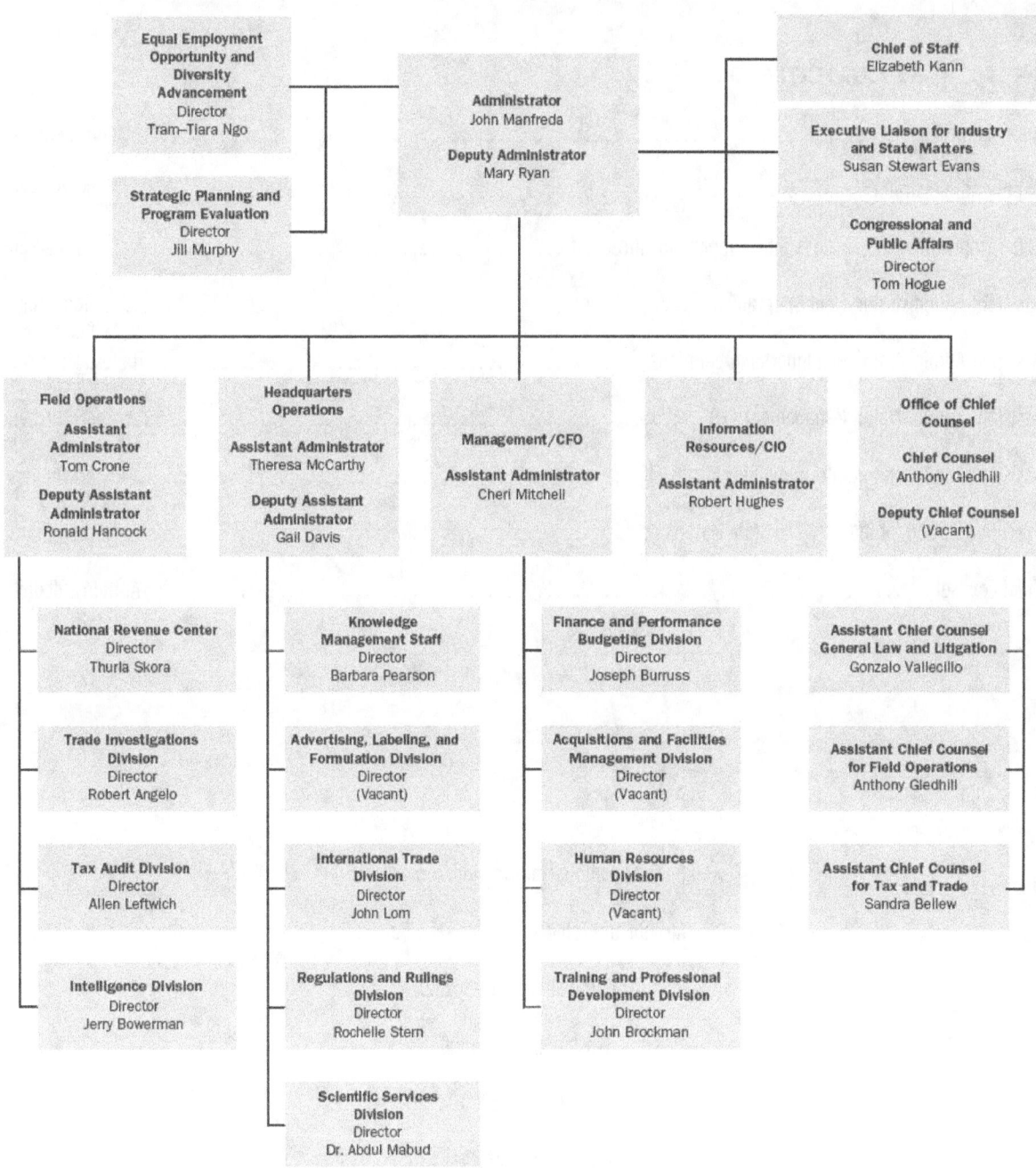

Equal Employment Opportunity and Diversity Advancement
Director
Tram–Tiara Ngo

Strategic Planning and Program Evaluation
Director
Jill Murphy

Administrator
John Manfreda

Deputy Administrator
Mary Ryan

Chief of Staff
Elizabeth Kann

Executive Liaison for Industry and State Matters
Susan Stewart Evans

Congressional and Public Affairs
Director
Tom Hogue

Field Operations
Assistant Administrator
Tom Crone
Deputy Assistant Administrator
Ronald Hancock

Headquarters Operations
Assistant Administrator
Theresa McCarthy
Deputy Assistant Administrator
Gail Davis

Management/CFO
Assistant Administrator
Cheri Mitchell

Information Resources/CIO
Assistant Administrator
Robert Hughes

Office of Chief Counsel
Chief Counsel
Anthony Gledhill
Deputy Chief Counsel
(Vacant)

National Revenue Center
Director
Thurla Skora

Knowledge Management Staff
Director
Barbara Pearson

Finance and Performance Budgeting Division
Director
Joseph Burruss

Assistant Chief Counsel General Law and Litigation
Gonzalo Vallecilio

Trade Investigations Division
Director
Robert Angelo

Advertising, Labeling, and Formulation Division
Director
(Vacant)

Acquisitions and Facilities Management Division
Director
(Vacant)

Assistant Chief Counsel for Field Operations
Anthony Gledhill

Tax Audit Division
Director
Allen Leftwich

International Trade Division
Director
John Lom

Human Resources Division
Director
(Vacant)

Assistant Chief Counsel for Tax and Trade
Sandra Bellew

Intelligence Division
Director
Jerry Bowerman

Regulations and Rulings Division
Director
Rochelle Stern

Training and Professional Development Division
Director
John Brockman

Scientific Services Division
Director
Dr. Abdul Mabud

Connecting the Treasury and TTB Strategic Plans

TREASURY GOALS	TTB STRATEGIC GOALS	TTB OBJECTIVES
TREASURY STRATEGIC GOAL: Enhance U.S. Competitiveness and Promote International Financial Stability and Balanced Global Growth **AGENCY PRIORITY GOAL:** Increase Electronic Transactions with the Public to Improve Service, Prevent Fraud, and Reduce Costs	**PROTECT THE PUBLIC (PTP):** Alcohol and tobacco industry operators meet permit qualifications, and alcohol beverage products comply with federal production, labeling, and marketing requirements	**PTP 1. BUSINESS INTEGRITY:** Assure that only qualified persons and business entities operate within the industries TTB regulates **PTP 2. PRODUCT INTEGRITY:** Assure that alcohol beverage products comply with federal production, labeling, and advertising requirements **PTP 3. MARKET INTEGRITY:** Assure fair trade practices throughout the alcohol beverage marketplace
TREASURY STRATEGIC GOAL: Pursue Comprehensive Tax and Fiscal Reform **AGENCY PRIORITY GOAL:** Increase Voluntary Tax Compliance	**COLLECT THE REVENUE (CTR):** Enforce the tax code to ensure proper federal tax payment on alcohol, tobacco, firearms, and ammunition products	**CTR 1. TAX VERIFICATION AND VALIDATION:** Assure voluntary compliance in the timely and accurate remittance of tax payments **CTR 2. CIVIL AND CRIMINAL ENFORCEMENT:** Detect and address noncompliance, excise tax evasion, and other criminal violations of the Internal Revenue Code in the industries TTB regulates
TREASURY STRATEGIC GOAL: Manage the Government's Finances in a Fiscally Responsible Manner **AGENCY PRIORITY GOAL:** Increase Electronic Transactions with the Public to Improve Service, Prevent Fraud, and Reduce Costs	**MANAGEMENT AND ORGANIZATIONAL EXCELLENCE (MGT):** Maximize performance, efficiency, and program results through effective resource and human capital management	**MGT 1. HUMAN CAPITAL MANAGEMENT:** Maintain a qualified, engaged, and satisfied workforce **MGT 2. TECHNOLOGY SOLUTIONS:** Deliver effective, streamlined, and flexible IT solutions that add value and support program performance **MGT 3. FINANCE AND PERFORMANCE RESULTS:** Facilitate strategic management and financial accountability through the delivery of timely and reliable financial and performance information

Note: TTB revised its goals and objectives in FY 2010, and is operating under these goals until the publication of its revised strategic plan in FY 2014. The current TTB strategic plan covers the period of FY 2007 – 2012.

Page left intentionally blank.

www.ttb.gov

www.ingramcontent.com/pod-product-compliance
Lightning Source LLC
Chambersburg PA
CBHW080259180526
45167CB00006B/2590